This book is dedicated to children around the world, particularly to young refugees who are innocent victims of war and violence.

Twenty percent of the author's royalties will go to the Tibetan Children's Village in Dharamsala, India.

ACKNOWLEDGEMENTS

Preparing a book for publication is like preparing for the birth of a child. Many people support the idea and your efforts, but only a few give generously of their time and advice.

Dr. Esther Eisenhower was one of these people. I am immensely appreciative of all the support and encouragement she has given me and greatly indebted to her for her constructive criticism upon reviewing the first draft of my book.

My warmest thanks go to Dr. Donna Kay Wright, who, as a principal and a nationally recognized educational administrator, supported my efforts as a teacher and contributed the Foreword to this book. I should also express my gratitude to Erik Pursehouse, Courtney Pelley, and Frank Bensinger, all most enabling administrators.

I appreciate the important contributions made by my colleagues. Many of the cooperative projects in Chapters Two and Three were developed with my dearest colleague and friend, Jeannette Bryant. Jim Blair, Alice Bransfield, Donna Carpenelli, Cynthia Eckert, Soon Kee Falkenstrom, Pam Freer, Franna Ruddell, and Joanne Schilling also contributed materials and creative ideas to the book. Allison Grader, Audrey Van Vliet, and Carol Williams were kind enough to take time out of their busy schedules to read one chapter each and to offer suggestions. I also wish to thank two colleagues with whom I was fortunate to teach and who share the same common bond of understanding ESL in a local and global context. They are Aagot Chand and Vinnie DiPietro.

I am grateful to my former teachers—Mademoiselle Beaumont, Mademoiselle Hugon, Madame Lucette Desvignes, and Monsieur Jean Talon—for their understanding instruction and guidance.

I am also indebted to my family for their help: to my husband, Erik, for his patience and support; to my daughter, Claire, for her suggestions and practical ideas; to my son, Michel-David, who inspired the segment on aviation in Volume 2; and most of all to my son, Jacques-Frédéric, who taught me how to use my computer.

My deep love and gratitude go out to all my students—past and present—for sharing their affection, their cultures, and their talents with me. Special thanks go to Evelin Lisseth Abarca, Sonya Khin, Lien Le, Cecilia Ortiz,and Sung-Won Yi for their artwork, to Stephan Strauss for his "Autumn" poem in Volume 1, and to Stanislava Uhrik for her "Peace" poem in Volume 2.

My students' collective gift, for which I am most grateful, is that they have afforded me glimpses into the true nature of the human condition and shown me the courage of children in the face of adversity.

Michelle De Cou-Landberg
Reston, Virginia

CONTENTS

Dedication, iii
Acknowledgments, iv
Contents, v
List of Reproducibles, vi
Foreword, vii
Introduction, viii

Chapter 1. Climates and Seasons: Watching the Weather, 1

Content Area Learning Web, 2; Sparking Interest, 3; Expanding Language, 7; Reading and Reflecting, 11; Creating and Sharing, 15; Getting Families Involved, 20; Suggested Readings, 22
Reproducible Masters, 25

Chapter 2. Trees and Plants: Our Rich, Green World, 31

Content Area Learning Web, 32; Sparking Interest, 33; Expanding Language, 36; Reading and Reflecting, 44; Creating and Sharing, 52; Getting Families Involved, 56; Suggested Readings, 57; Reproducible Masters, 60

Chapter 3. Animals Around the World: Tame, Wild, or Mythical, 65

Content Area Learning Web, 66; Sparking Interest, 67; Expanding Language, 69; Reading and Reflecting, 74; Creating and Sharing, 82; Getting Families Involved, 87; Suggested Readings, 89; Reproducible Masters, 93

Chapter 4. International Foods: From Frijoles to Dal, 103

Content Area Learning Web, 104; Sparking Interest, 105; Expanding Language, 107; Reading and Reflecting, 113; Creating and Sharing, 120; Getting Families Involved, 124; Suggested Readings, 126; Reproducible Masters, 129

LIST OF REPRODUCIBLES

Chapter 1. Climates and Seasons

My Weather Calendar, 25
Comparatives and Superlatives, 26
Lisseth's Weather Graph, 27
What is the Weather Like? 28
Global Weather Watch, 29
Cloud Outline, 30

Chapter 2. Trees and Plants

Matching Leaves, 60
Fruits and Vegetables from My Country, 61
Find the Roots, 62
Azadeh's Geranium, 63
Trees and Plants, 64

Chapter 3. Animals Around the World

Animals from My Country, 93
Things Animals Do, 94
Things Animals Have, 95
Comparatives and Superlatives, 96
Animal Booklet (6 pages), 97–102

Chapter 4. International Foods

Sorting Foods, 129
Sweet/Sour Chart, 130
Opposites, 131
Hamud's Bag and Basket, 132
Rukhamini's Favorite Fruit, 133
Table of Facts, 134

The pages listed here may be reproduced for classroom use.

FOREWORD

When I accepted a position as principal of Haycock Elementary School in 1980, I expected to be greeted by the kinds of students found in most suburban Washington, D.C. neighborhoods. I soon discovered, however, that Haycock was not a typical suburban school. It had been designated a magnet school for the county's ESL program. The children came from all over the world and spoke 15 different languages. Some of their parents were from diplomatic families, while others had reached the U.S. via refugee camps where they had experienced horrors most people cannot even imagine.

How could we meet the special needs of such a diverse ESL population and, at the same time, help the native speakers in the school gain from this unique opportunity to learn more about the world? The answer to this question came from an exceptional ESL teacher, Michelle De Cou-Landberg. She devised completely original lessons based on the needs and resources of each student.

But Michelle did more than just teach English. She arranged a presentation on Japanese writing for the whole school. She organized the production and sale of an international cookbook and put together a Children's International Festival. Her activities helped students, parents, and teachers to understand and appreciate more deeply each others' cultures.

The Global Classroom contains the essence of what Michelle brought to Haycock. It is full of classroom suggestions, but it also contains many ideas for bringing together ESL students, non-ESL students, teachers, families, and the community in an environment that will help everyone learn to live and work together. I commend Michelle for her extraordinary service to children from all lands and cultures and for her contribution to the growth of global education.

D. Kay Wright
United States Department of Education
Mid-Atlantic Region

INTRODUCTION

The Global Classroom is child-centered.

- It provides for a setting in which all contributions are valued and all experiences are meaningful.
- It seeks to develop a supportive environment in which the student is nurtured and develops a positive self-image.
- It helps children learn about, appreciate, and celebrate the differences and the commonalities of the world's many cultures.

The Global Classroom consists of two volumes. Volume 1 consists of four chapters, each of which addresses a universal theme: weather, plants, animals, and food. Each chapter provides a wide variety of exercises to capture students' interest, expand their language abilities, motivate them to read, and show them how to share the learning process with their families. All activities can be used in a variety of settings and can be adapted to a wide range of age and proficiency levels. Volume 2 of *The Global Classroom* follows a similar format and includes chapters on clothing, housing, transportation, and celebrations.

The first four sections of each chapter (Sparking Interest, Expanding Language, Reading and Reflecting, and Creating and Sharing) contain activities and strategies which address the issues of multi-level grouping, classroom management, and collaborative learning. The fifth section, Getting Families Involved, gives suggestions for helping include students' families in the education and acculturation process. The sixth section, Suggested Readings, contains a listing of multicultural children's books which focus on the chapter theme. The last section of each chapter contains reproducible masters which can be duplicated for classroom use.

Sparking Interest

In the Sparking Interest section you will find suggestions for generating interest in the theme. Considerable aural and visual materials are used so that students have a chance to listen and watch. They are also encouraged to use the senses of touch, smell, and taste as ways of getting to know more about the theme.

Expanding Language

In this section, activities focus on building vocabulary, improving pronunciation, and figuring out how the grammar of English works. All activities grow out of the context provided by the chapter theme, and all classwork involves real, meaningful communication.

Reading and Reflecting

In this section, students take a look at some books relating to the theme. Big Books are often used at the beginning of this section to provide a whole-group reading activity. Then, beginning level students may listen to the teacher read stories and respond by drawing a picture or writing a few words. More advanced students may read on their own in groups. Specific books and follow-up activities are listed along with original projects.

Creating and Sharing

In this section, students work on art projects, do further research into some aspect of the theme, write or deliver oral reports, publish booklets, and carry out hands-on science projects.

Getting Families Involved

The suggestions in this section have several purposes. One is to let the family know what the student is learning so that they can provide emotional support. A second purpose is to draw on the resources students' families can provide for the class as a whole. When family members share aspects of their culture (such as food, art, or music) with the class, all students are drawn closer together and communication is enhanced. A third function of these suggestions is to give non-English-speaking family members some exposure to the language.

Suggested Readings

Each chapter ends with a list of theme-related titles which can be used to expand and enrich activities. A bullet (•) appears next to any title which is also featured in the chapter. These featured titles are not required readings, but are used to illustrate the literature-based activities. You may wish to substitute another book related to the theme from this list, or from your classroom or library collection.

Reproducibles

Each chapter contains a set of reproducible masters which accompany some of the suggested activities. Teachers are encouraged to use the ideas presented in these reproducibles to construct new versions tailored to the needs of a particular class.

Each chapter provides a wide variety of choices from which you can construct your own sequence of instruction. Many of the activities can be applied across the themes, adapted to different levels of students, and built upon or recreated by you or your students. You may choose to spend as little or as much time on any section or theme as you wish, integrate and expand activities, or become inspired to create entirely new activities. The material is presented as a springboard for creativity, with the needs and interests of your students as your guide.

In the margin of each page you will find three types of entries: Notes, Materials, and Readings. The Notes provide special insights and suggestions for expanding on an activity. A Materials list is provided when an activity requires materials beyond those commonly found in the classroom. Reading lists highlight the books featured in literature-based activities. (Detailed publication information for these books can be found in the Suggested Readings section of each chapter.)

The materials presented in *The Global Classroom* reflect the author's experiences as a French student learning English as a "living language" (langue vivante); as an EFL teacher in France and Laos; as an observer of literacy projects in Nepal and schools in India; and as an ESL teacher in Fairfax County, Virginia. There are more activities here than any teacher could ever cover in school year—activities to help you teach exciting, inviting, child-centered classes. Feel free to pick and choose, to imitate, to innovate. Use *The Global Classroom* not only to teach English, but also to celebrate the cultural diversity of your students.

CLIMATES AND SEASONS
Chapter
1
WATCHING THE WEATHER

CONTENT AREA LEARNING WEB

CLIMATES AND SEASONS

SCIENCE

Recording the weather on a calendar, 4

Reading a thermometer and recording temperatures, 5, 7

Learning to understand weather forecasts, 5, 10

Taking a Nature Walk, 7

Drawing conclusions from Nature Walk observations, 7

Observing clouds, 9

Making weather predictions, 9

Discussing how winds affect climate, 11

Comparing different seasons, 16

MATH

Recording temperatures on a graph, 5

Practicing weather-related math terms, 9

Comparing Fahrenheit and Celsius systems, 9

Tracking the weather on a graph, 9

LANGUAGE ARTS

Using weather vocabulary with a calendar, 4

Onomatopoeia: imitating weather sounds, 6

Discussing seasonal sensations, 6, 15

Adjectives, 7

Expressing observations, 7

Writing descriptive sentences, 7

Comparatives and superlatives, 8, 15

Verb tenses, 8

Weather Watch Web, 10

Weather Watch Brainstorm, 10

Describing the weather in different countries, 10, 13–14, 16

Differentiating adjectives from nouns, 11, 14

Categorizing weather words, 14

Weather word search, 17

Writing weather stories and poems, 18

Making an events chart, 18–20

Studying -er words, 20

SOCIAL STUDIES

Researching temperatures in other countries, 5

Taking a Nature Walk, 7

Discussing seasons around the globe, 9

Comparing temperature-recording systems, 9

Describing the weather in different countries, 10, 12, 13

Learning about winds around the world, 11

Understanding the impact of weather on rural life, 13

Describing weather-related activities, 16

ART AND MUSIC

Weather songs, sounds, and music, 6

Making weather/seasonal drawings, 6, 12, 15, 16

Illustrating Nature Walk observations, 7

Illustrating weather words, 15

Making and displaying kites, 16

Illustrating colloquial expressions, 17

Making weather booklets, 18

Making a timeline, 20

READING COMPREHENSION

Learning to understand weather forecasts, 5

Listening for specific content, 12

Predicting story endings, 12

Picking out weather expressions, 13

FAMILY INVOLVEMENT

Interviewing families, 21

Comparing weather expressions from different countries, 21

Comparing weather vocabulary, 21

Learning about seasonal activities in different countries, 21

CHAPTER 1. CLIMATES AND SEASONS

En avril,
ne te découvre pas d'un fil;
en mai,
fais ce qu'il te plaît.

In April,
don't take off a single thread;
in May,
do as you please.

—OLD FRENCH SAYING

This is a good chapter to use at the beginning of the school year. A unit on the weather and seasons around the world will encourage the sharing of universal experiences. Invite students to open their eyes, their ears, their mouths, their hands, and their minds as you embark on a discovery of the world together.

In any language, the ability to discuss the weather is a valuable social skill and a valid measure of language proficiency. An unseasoned French student will say "Il pleut beaucoup," whereas a student more familiar with the language will venture "Il pleut à verse." In English, "It's raining cats and dogs" is a lot more interesting than "It's raining." In Spanish, "Llueve mucho" is more basic than "Llueve a cántaros." In German, "Es regnet in Strömen" is more descriptive than "Es regnet."

A unit on the weather can act as a springboard for a variety of discussions and activities. The topic can also be recycled throughout the year since weather is a cyclical, global concept—one that affects our daily lives and the lives of several billion other inhabitants of our fragile planet.

SPARKING INTEREST

This section is filled with ideas to help your students get off to a good start. It describes a variety of materials and activities that can inspire them to use their senses—sight, hearing, smell, and touch—to learn more about the weather and the seasons.

The bulletin board can become an especially important focus. It gives students a place to see their most recent drawings and stories prominently displayed. It also gives them a convenient way to share any visual or written materials they discover that relate to the theme. Wall calendars and other types of charts can be obtained from a teacher's supply store, or produced by the teacher and students.

Using Visual Stimuli

Setting up a Wall Calendar

- Place a wall calendar in a prominent place on the bulletin board at the entrance of the classroom.
- Attach a colored construction paper strip to show what month it is.
- Use colored construction paper to make pictures to place on the calendar: school buses in September, autumn leaves in October, pumpkins in November, etc.
- Make small picture cards showing several types of weather.
- Make similar picture cards showing the four seasons.
- Laminate all materials, if possible, for longer use.

Some Weather Pictures

Activities with a Wall Calendar

MATERIALS
- ✓ *cardboard or posterboard*
- ✓ *crayons or markers*
- ✓ *clothespins*
- ✓ *"My Weather Calendar" reproducible master, page 25*

- During the first week of school discuss students' responsibilities and decide on weekly tasks. Who will pass out papers, wash the board, change the date on the calendar, record the weather, etc.? Make a sign depicting each job on a piece of cardboard or posterboard. Write students' names on wooden clothespins which can be clipped to each sign and easily rotated each week.
- At the beginning of the unit, teach and review calendar and weather vocabulary. You can have one student place a numbered school bus on the current day of the week on the wall calendar, and then ask the rest of the class to draw a symbol showing what the weather is like in the corresponding blank in their own calendar. Make copies of "My Weather Calendar" on page 25 and distribute them to all students. Show them how to keep their own record of the weather by entering the date, one of the weather symbols from the top of the page, and the temperature each day.

Activities for Beginning and Intermediate Students

Once your students feel comfortable with the daily calendar routine, you might want to expand it by recording the weather and including some math practice in the process. The following section includes activities for both beginning and intermediate students. Vary the activities according to the ability levels of the students.

MATERIALS
- ✓ sturdy outdoor thermometer
- ✓ graph paper
- ✓ newspaper weather reports

Keeping Track of the Weather

- If possible, hang a sturdy thermometer outside the classroom window.
- Teach students how to read a thermometer and write temperatures on the board
- Add "meteorologist" to the list of weekly jobs and teach students how to record temperatures on a separate graph like the one pictured below.
- Ask students to listen to the weather forecast.
- Bring newspaper weather reports to school.
- Show students how to find out the daily temperature in their native countries and record it on their graph.

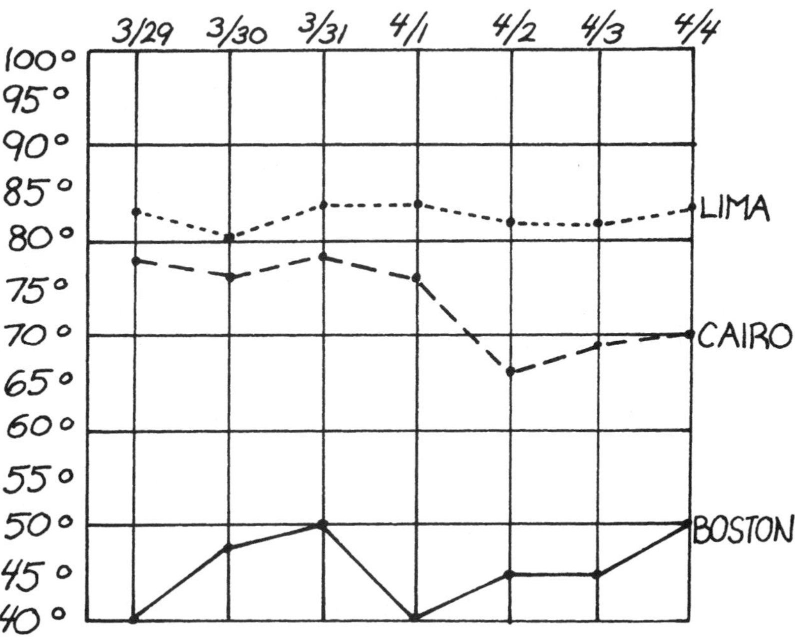

A Temperature Graph

MATERIALS

✓ *recording of* The Four Seasons *by Antonio Vivaldi*
✓ *recordings of environments and weather sounds*

Using Auditory Stimuli

- Explain onomatopoeia. Have students imitate the sounds of rain, thunder, a windstorm, etc.
- Ask students to sing songs about the weather from their native countries and then explain or draw pictures about each song.
- Play a tape of *The Four Seasons* by Antonio Vivaldi. Ask students to guess which part of the music represents which season.
- Bring in environmental tapes which capture the sounds of wind, rain, the ocean, and a pond at night. Ask students to talk about the seasons and kinds of weather each sound reminds them of.

Using Kinesthetic Stimuli

- From time to time open the classroom window and observe the changing of the seasons. Ask students to talk about how the air feels, what the wind smells like, etc.

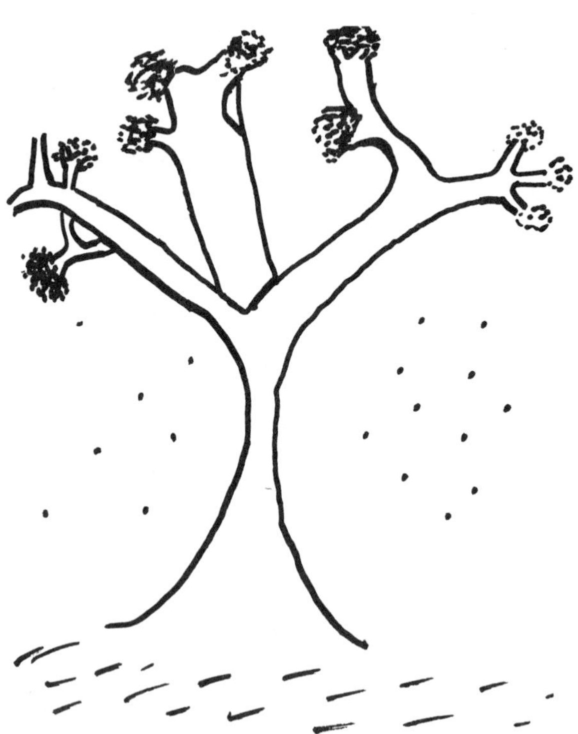

Something I saw on the Nature Walk
Evelin Lisseth Abarca, Age 10

- Take Nature Walks several times throughout the year. Encourage students to feel, smell, and touch the flowers and trees. Ask them to notice the feel of the rain, the snow, or the air.
- Invite students to observe the birds and other animals, the position of the sun, the cloud formations, etc. Ask them what each of these elements tells us about the seasons and the weather.
- Encourage students to draw simple pictures of their impressions.

EXPANDING LANGUAGE

At this point, you have aroused the students' interest and introduced them to the basic concepts and language needed to talk about the weather and the seasons. Here are some ideas that allow students to build on what they have learned as they interact with each other while doing whole-class, group, and paired activities.

Using Adjectives

Students will learn to use a variety of descriptive adjectives as they experience and talk about the weather. They may encounter such terms as *hot, humid, muggy, sultry, warm, mild, comfortable, cool, crisp,* and *chilly.*

MATERIALS

✓ *completed student weather calendars*

- Help newcomers to communicate with others as they answer simple questions about the weather using their own calendars as stimuli.
- Help students ask and answer questions like these: *How is the weather?* (It's warm and muggy.) *What is the weather like today?* (It's chilly.) *Is it sunny?* (No, it's cloudy.) *Is it cold?* (It's not cold, but it's cool.)
- Impress the meteorologist of the week with the importance of his or her job. Help this person read the thermometer and record the temperature on the board. Encourage the use of complete sentences. For example: *Today is a sunny day. It is 53 degrees Fahrenheit. It is warmer than yesterday.*

APRIL						
S.	M.	T.	W.	TH.	FRI.	SAT.
1 70°F	2 60°F	3 80°F	4 95°F	5 70°F	6 65°F	7 60°F
8 60°F	9 70°F	10 65°F	11 75°F	12 90°F	13 100°F	14 80°F

A Weather Calendar

- Practice the comparatives and superlatives: *Is today sunnier than yesterday? Which day was warmer—Tuesday or Thursday? What was the hottest day this month? Which country has the hottest weather in October—Vietnam or Bolivia?*

MATERIALS

✓ *"Comparatives and Superlatives" reproducible master, page 26*
✓ The Guinness Book of Records, *edited by Peter Matthews*

- Make copies of "Comparatives and Superlatives" on page 26 and distribute them to students who can benefit from written practice with these language items.
- For further practice with superlatives, encourage students to use the *Guinness Book of Records* to look up and report to the class on the fastest runner, the biggest birthday cake, the smallest human being, and other interesting information involving extremes.

Using Verbs

- Give students realistic practice with verb tenses: *When was it sunny last week? What was the weather like on September 16th? Did you need an umbrella on the 10th?*

Communicating about Content Areas

- Use this opportunity to point to a world map or globe and explain why autumn begins in the Northern Hemisphere at the same time that spring begins in the Southern Hemisphere.

- Practice using mathematical terms: *Which day had the highest temperature? Which day had the lowest temperature? What is the difference between the two?* Children will be able to grasp this concept as early as first grade.
- Older students may wish to compare how many countries use the Fahrenheit system and how many use the Celsius system. Ask students to take a class survey and make a color-coded graph. How many students are familiar with degrees centigrade? Which countries do they come from? How many use the Fahrenheit system? Where are they from? Which is the easier system? Why?

MATERIALS
✓ *graph paper and pencils*
✓ *Science Learning Logs*

- Ask students to watch clouds and draw them in Science Learning Logs, if they have them.
- By using all available resources and observing nature, students will begin to make accurate weather predictions. Start discussions using questions like these: *What will the weather be like tomorrow? How do you know? What makes you say that?*

MATERIALS
✓ *"Lisseth's Weather Graph" reproducible master, page 27*

- Make copies of "Lisseth's Weather Graph" on page 27 and distribute them to students who are ready to read information from a simple graph and answer some questions about it. Beginning level students may give one-word answers, while more advanced children may be able to respond in complete sentences. Have students write their answers in their notebooks.
- The concept of seasons is difficult for some students to understand. As the class observes the cycle of seasons in your area, compare and contrast them with the seasons the students experienced in their native countries. Possible questions include: *What kinds of clothes do they wear in hot weather in Korea? What kind of clothes do they wear when it's cold in Czechoslovakia? Have you ever seen a sandstorm? What happens when a monsoon comes? Are there floods in Bangladesh when it rains hard? What happens to the soil?*
- Ask students what they know about a rainstorm. As a class, make a Weather Watch Web about rainstorms like the one

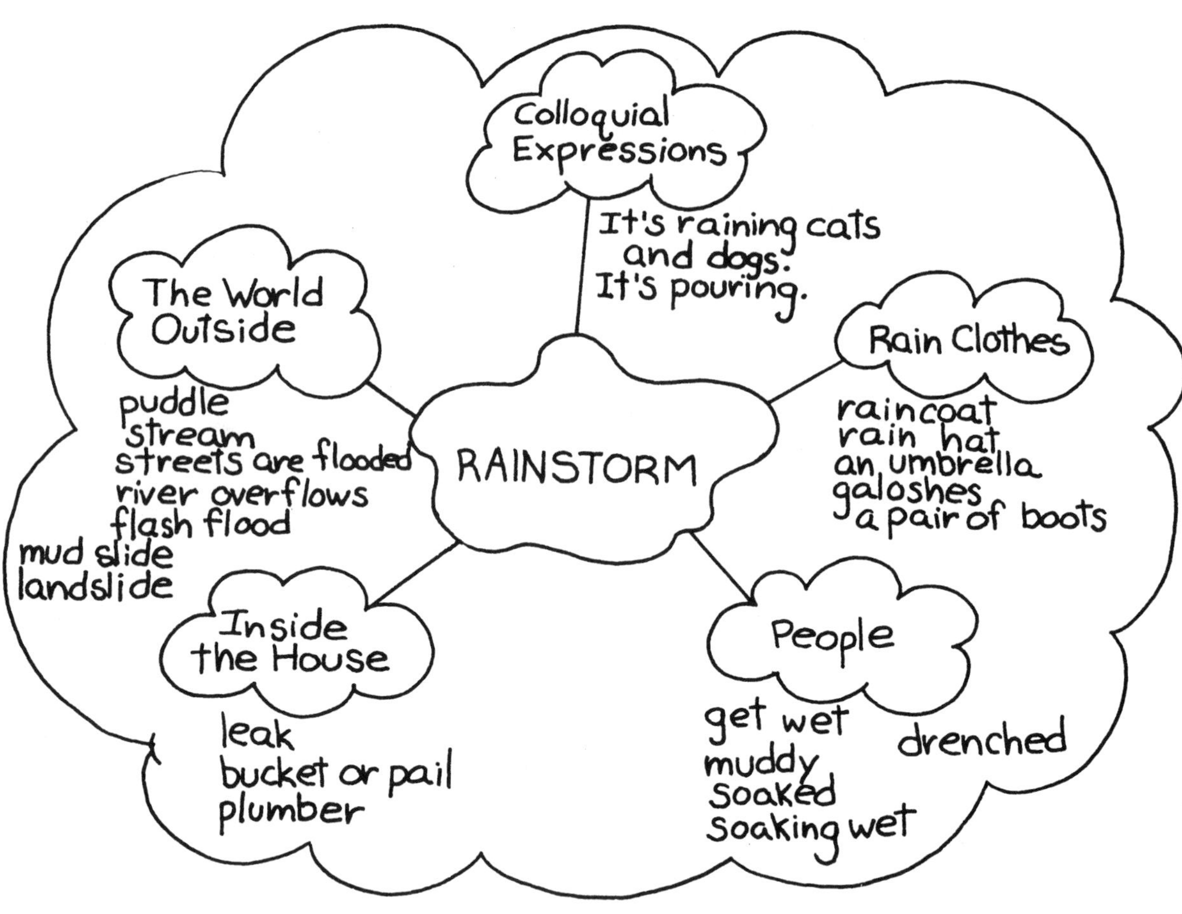

Weather Watch Web

above. Post the Weather Watch Web on the bulletin board. Encourage students to add their own contributions whenever they wish.

NOTE *Webbing and brainstorming are excellent follow-up activities and may be adapted for all ages and language proficiency levels.*

- Intermediate or advanced level students can engage in generating vocabulary about different kinds of storms using a Weather Watch Brainstorm like the one on the following page. A mini-lesson on compound words can follow.
- Ask advanced level students to locate a specific country on a map or globe and describe the weather there.
- For a good listening exercise, give students the local weather number and ask them to listen to the weather forecast each morning or evening. Discuss the report in class. Add new words and expressions to your web and post them on the bulletin board for future reference.
- Make copies of "What is the Weather Like?" on page 28 and

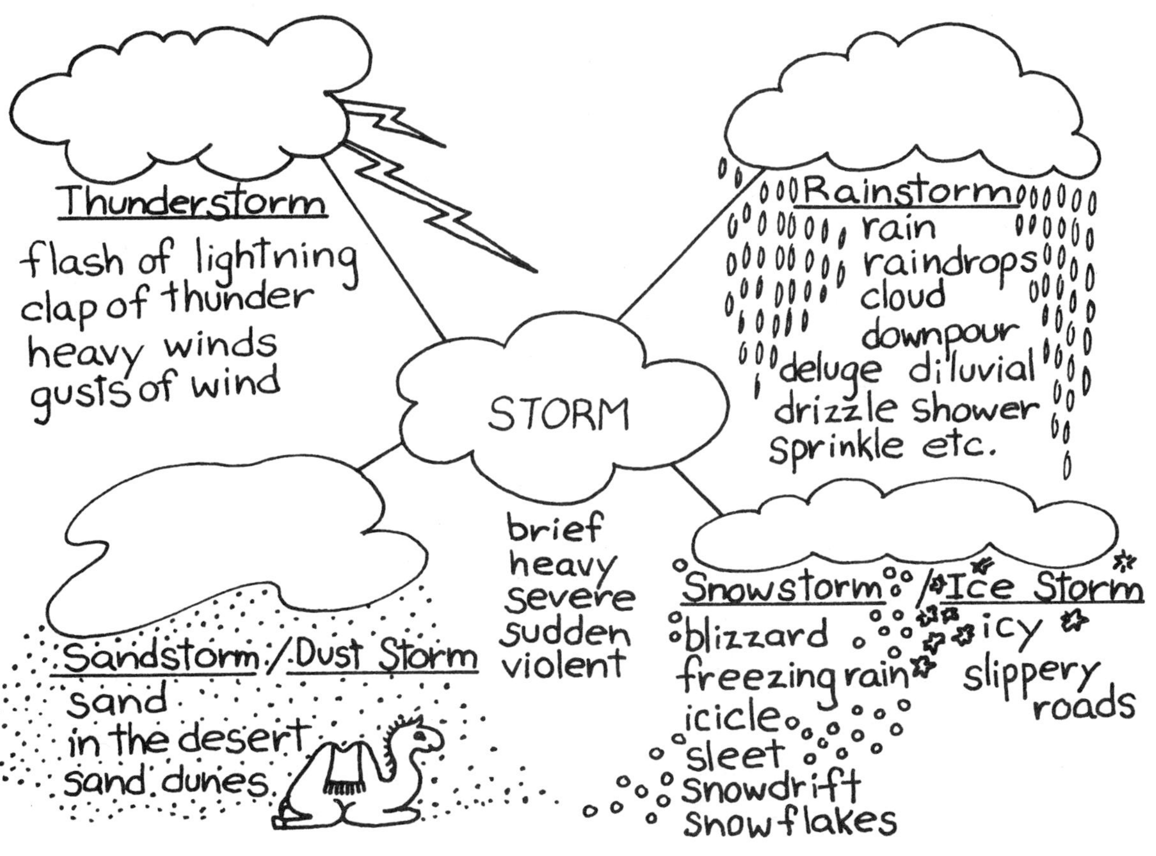

Weather Watch Brainstorm

MATERIALS

✓ *"What is the Weather Like?" reproducible master, page 28*

distribute them to students who can benefit from practice differentiating between adjectives and nouns.

- Brainstorm with students a list of names of some of the winds that blow in their part of the world and how these winds affect the climate. A partial list might include: el niño, Al-Khamsin, el sirocco, der Föhn, la tramontana, le mistral, and les alizés.

READING AND REFLECTING

Now that the vocabulary has been introduced and developed and the concepts presented, students are ready to go on to the next step. The first two sections below help them relate what they have learned to stories you read together in class. These activities are followed by a variety of suggestions which allow students to explore some topics even further. The following descriptions show what I have done in the past. You can use your imagination to devise similar activities for any of the hundreds of other stories available to you.

Using Multicultural Literature

✓ Rani, Queen of the Jungle, *by Constantine Giorgiou*

READING

- Read aloud *Rani, Queen of the Jungle,* by Constantine Giorgiou. In this story a young Indian boy named Krishna wants a real jungle animal for a friend. Soon his wish is fulfilled as an old hermit lays a bundle on the doorstep. He receives a little tiger cub wrapped in dusty rags. The author's poetic language captures the sweet scent of the earth, the rainy monsoon days, the bright sunlight, the roar of the jungle and the changing of seasons as the tiger cub grows and begins to yearn for freedom.
- As you read aloud to the students, ask them to raise their hands when they hear a reference to the weather or seasons.
- Ask students to draw clues from the illustrations to help them predict the ending of the story.

✓ Bringing the Rain to Kapiti Plain, *by Verna Aardema*

READING

- Read *Bringing the Rain to Kapiti Plain,* a tale from Kenya retold by Verna Aardema and illustrated by Beatriz Vidal. Talk about the illustrations and discuss the story. Compare the weather, vegetation, and animals to those the students are familiar with. Give students a long strip of recycled computer paper. (Plain, white shelf paper cut in two works well, too.) Ask students to illustrate the weather in the story: the heavy black clouds hanging over the brown ground, the cloud pierced by Ki-Pat's arrow, the flashes of lightning, the heavy raindrops, and the green grass. Even beginning level students will be able to visualize the landscape and understand how the weather affects the vegetation, animals, and people.

Using American Literature

- *Cloudy with a Chance of Meatballs,* by Judy Barrett, is a tall tale incorporating weather and foods. It works well with intermediate and advanced levels, and lends itself to a number of activities, especially a follow-up on tall tales. The following weather expressions are gleaned from the book.

✓ Cloudy with a Chance of Meatballs, *by Judy Barrett*

READING

- Cloudy, with a chance of...
- weather report
- prediction/forecast
- a brief shower
- low clouds
- sprinkle/drizzle
- becoming heavy at times
- periods of ____ followed by gradual clearing
- pea soup fog
- violent storm
- hurricane
- drifts
- tornado
- damage

Book Talk Activities

Use collaborative "Book Talk" groups to help students learn new vocabulary, discuss new ideas, reinforce old concepts, and analyze what they have read. The Suggested Readings section at the end of this chapter provides a partial list of multicultural books well suited to learning about the weather and the seasons, but the possibilities are endless.

✓ Little House in the Big Woods, *by Laura Ingalls Wilder*

✓ Little House on the Prairie, *by Laura Ingalls Wilder*

READING

- As students read trade books in small groups, ask them to focus on the weather and cycle of seasons. *Little House in the Big Woods* and *Little House on the Prairie,* by Laura Ingalls Wilder, are books which work well with intermediate and advanced students in grades 4-6. Most students like them a lot, perhaps because a great number of them come from rural areas and agrarian societies.
- A group of low intermediate students might study the description of a storm and present their collective findings, along with a vocabulary list, to the rest of the class.
- Advanced students reading the Little House books might decide on the chapter they feel provides the best description of a certain type of weather and analyze it for vocabulary and content with their respective groups.
- As a culminating activity, you might ask students to compare and contrast the weather in the area described in the book they have read with the weather in their native countries or in a certain part of that country.

MATERIALS

✓ "Global Weather Watch" reproducible master, page 29

- Give each student a copy of "Global Weather Watch" on page 29 as a source of possible vocabulary words to use during this assignment. You will see your class's awareness of weather worldwide increase tremendously as a result of these assignments and discussions. And you'll be delighted by the input you'll get from all of your students!

Enrichment Activities

The following activities can be used as homework, group work, or independent study.

MATERIALS

✓ "Global Weather Watch" reproducible master, page 29

✓ index cards

- Practice the vocabulary on the "Global Weather Watch" reproducible master. Ask students to color code the nouns and adjectives.
- Have students copy the Global Weather Watch words on index cards and categorize them according to season, type of weather, etc.

Sonya (Su) Khin, Age 11

- Select six to ten basic words and ask beginning level students to illustrate them and to write a sentence for each word.

NOTE

Ask the librarian to loan you a supply of handy reference books for these activities. If possible, keep them in your classroom for a few days.

- Ask students to do some research to find the rainiest, the coldest, the driest, or the windiest place on earth. Or assign specific questions such as *What is the average annual rainfall in Bahrain?*

CREATING AND SHARING

Throughout your weather studies, allow students some time to create their own products related to the theme, including drawings, charts, and stories. Encourage them to talk about their findings with their partners. A number of activities will arise from these experiences.

Activities for Beginning Level Students

A Nature Walk

MATERIALS

✓ *audio taping equipment*

- After a short walk outdoors (perhaps in the snow on the first snowy day of the season) tape record the students' animated comments. Taping students serves two purposes: it provides the children with feedback and motivation; it is also an excellent way of measuring oral proficiency progress over time.
- Brainstorm snow vocabulary with students and write the results on the board.
- Give students some drawing paper and ask them to draw a weather-related picture. This way, even recently arrived students can feel pride in their work and can feel very much a part of the group despite their limited knowledge of English.
- Provide students with chalk and encourage them to draw a mural on the chalkboard together entitled "A Snowy Day."

Art and Writing Activities

- Recycle computer paper by folding it in half lengthwise and asking students to illustrate the walk they took, the change of seasons, or any other weather-related topic. Students may wish to write a few sentences to accompany their drawings.

- Have students divide sheets of paper into four equal rectangles by folding it in half horizontally and then vertically. Ask them to number the four rectangles and draw pictures illustrating the four seasons.
- Encourage them to do the same for the seasons in their native countries or for other countries they are familiar with. Are the seasons the same? Do they occur in the same months as those in the local area?
- Ask students to describe their favorite season and tell why they like it so much. What activities do they enjoy in this season? What are their favorite winter sports?
- Ask students to make booklets showing activities frequently associated with specific seasons, such as swimming in a pool, collecting brightly-colored leaves, making a snowman, shoveling snow, etc.

READING

✓ Ramu and the Kite, *by Mehlli Gobhai*

✓ The Dragon Kite, *by Thomas P. Lewis*

✓ *other books about kites*

Using Literature

- Read *Ramu and the Kite,* by Mehlli Gobhai (or another book about kites) and help the children build their own kites. This experience will give students a chance to feel first-hand the power of the wind. *The Dragon Kite,* by Thomas P. Lewis, provides an interesting parallel to the first book. It is about another eight-year-old boy, a Tibetan child named Kesang, who goes to Lhasa and flies over the city in a kite.
- After reading one of these books, discuss the kite season in the students' native countries and in your local area and invite students to make their own kites and bring them for display in the classroom. There are many types of kites for students to make. Try leaving them on their own for this project. You may be surprised at the talent and ingenuity the children and their families exhibit!

Activities for Intermediate and Advanced Students

Idiomatic Expressions

- Discuss the following expressions and invite students to use terms they encounter in their reading to expand the list. Ask each student to illustrate one of the expressions on an 8½-by-11-inch piece of paper. Create a colorful bulletin board using these drawings.

Expressions describing weather

- It's raining cats and dogs.
- to be under the weather
- nothing new under the sun
- It's coming down in buckets.
- April showers bring May flowers.
- Save it for a rainy day.
- rain or shine
- to be on Cloud Nine
- a pelting rain
- a fair weather friend

Sonya (Su) Khin, Age 11

Word Search. Have students write as many words as they can using only the letters in the word *weather.* This activity serves as a good "sponge." Here are a few examples: *we, he, war, at, wreath, the, tar, there, thaw, tear, ear, hate, her, ate, rat, wear, rate, threw, tea, raw,* and *water.*

Writing Activities

- Make a copy of the cloud outline on page 30 for each student. Ask them to use it as a book cover and cut out more pages of the same shape to attach to the cover. Then have

MATERIALS

✓ *the cloud outline reproducible master, page 30*

NOTE

This activity would be especially appropriate after reading Cloudy with a Chance of Meatballs, *by Judy Barrett.*

them fill in the cloud-shaped pages with stories, either real or imaginary. Possible topics include:

• Describe the rainy (summer, winter, etc.) season in your native country. Compare and contrast it with the weather in the local area. Which one do you like best? Why?

• Write about ways that the weather affects people's lives (droughts, storms, effects on types of clothing worn or homes lived in, etc.) How can weather be helpful? How can it be harmful? Can we control the weather?

When students have finished, ask them to think of a title for their book and write it on the cover along with their own names.

- Write an acrostics poem entitled *First Day of Autumn.* Here is a sample of what this kind of poem looks like. This one is by a former student of mine, Stephan Strauss.

A Acorns are delicious to squirrels.
U Umbrellas are beautiful and keep me dry.
T Two pine cones look like the ears of a rabbit.
U Under the leaves, insects are crawling.
M Maple leaves are like flames of fire.
N Nature is beautiful in the fall.

Making an Events Chart

READING

✓ A New Coat for Anna, *by Harriet Ziefert*

- *A New Coat for Anna,* by Harriet Ziefert, can serve as a starting point for class discussion and writing about the seasons of the year. It tells the story of the steps Anna and her mother go through in order to obtain the materials needed to make a new coat for the little girl. As the seasons pass, they encounter various workers (the sheep farmer, the spinner, etc.) and trade a variety of objects for the materials and services that are needed to make the coat.
- To help students follow the story and recall the sequence of events, bring in as many of the actual objects mentioned in the book as possible: wool, berries, red cloth, etc.
- After you have read and discussed the book, draw a circle on large drawing paper and create a chart showing the events of the year. (See the illustration below.) This representation of

time works better than a timeline for this story. Ask students to recall the most important events in the story and the main trading objects. Then have them draw simple pictures to represent the most important events, and write short phrases describing the objects that were traded throughout the story. Students can then write original stories using the cycle of seasons as an organizing principle.

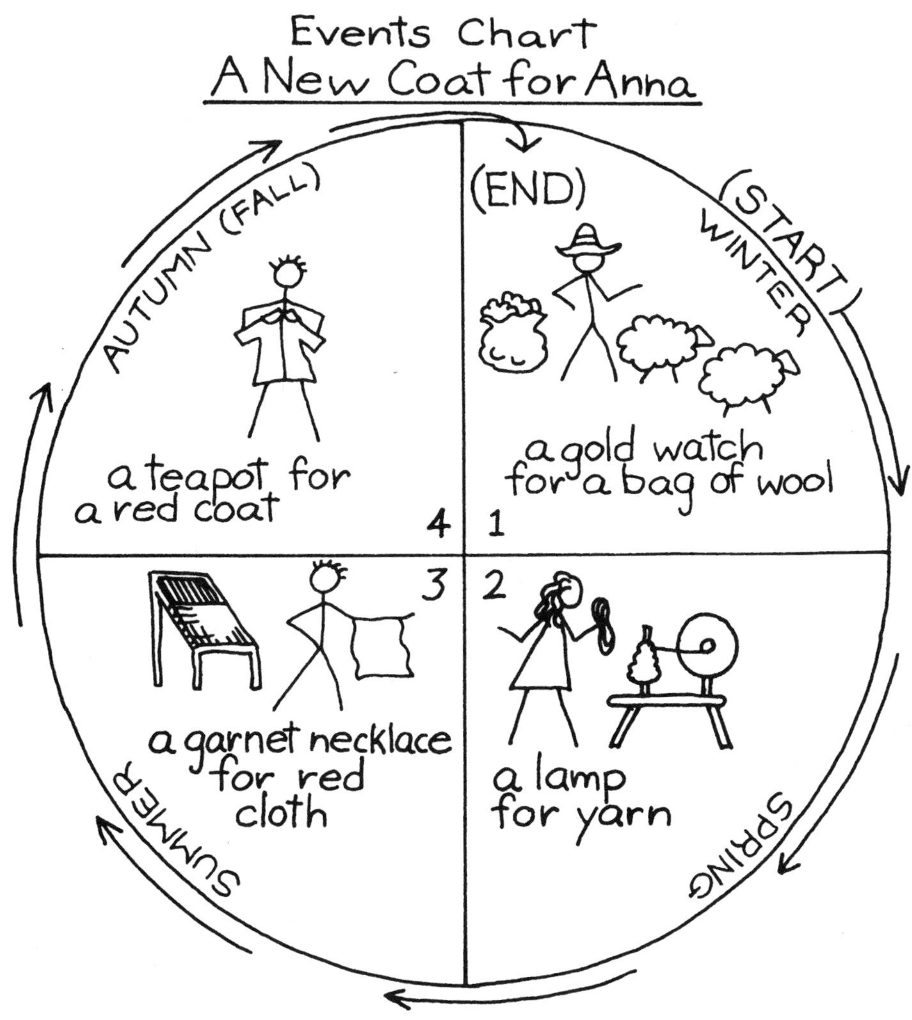

- Invite students to rewrite the story from Anna's point of view, from the point of view of one of the other people in the story, or from the sheep's point of view.
- Publish the stories either in the form of a single class book, or as a series of small individual books which the students illustrate themselves.

✓ We are Navajo, *by Judith Sullivan*

READING

- You might wish to contrast the events in this story with those in *We are Navajo,* by Judith Sullivan, comparing the Navajo and European lifestyles.
- If you wish, you may conduct a mini-lesson on occupations featuring nouns ending in *-er,* such as *farmer, weaver,* and *spinner.*

✓ The Little Red Hen *(any version)*

READING

- There are a variety of other stories that follow a series of events through the seasons of the year which you can use for this kind of activity. Very young students might enjoy the story of *The Little Red Hen* who plants, cares for, and harvests the wheat, and eventually makes it into bread.

Making a Traditional Timeline

Since so many of the charts and graphic representations are circular, a more traditional timeline for the Global Classroom can provide a welcome change and brighten the walls. It can also help you teach past, present, and future expressions, using as reference points dates and events of significance to your students.

MATERIALS

✓ *construction paper and crayons or markers*
✓ *string to hang pictures from*
✓ *paper clips or clothes-pins*

- Use 8½-by-11-inch construction paper and begin a timeline of important dates. Begin with Labor Day and the first day of school. After that, choose other important dates based on the students' cultures, the curriculum, the weather, etc.
- Ask students to illustrate each event.
- Hang the timeline on a cord suspended from the ceiling and refer to it often to practice talking about past, present, and future events.

GETTING FAMILIES INVOLVED

Families are the link between the place students left behind and their new world. In some cases, particularly with refugees, the experience of leaving home has been shattering, and they may find it hard to adjust to the new lifestyles and customs. Some families have little free time to help their children with home-work. Family members may be illiterate. One way to make families feel valued is to invite them to share their oral traditions and customs with their children, and therefore, with the school.

Researching Weather and Seasons at Home

- Have students ask their families to explain, or remind them of, the cycle of seasons in their country of origin.
- Students can also work with their families to draw charts or pictures of weather in their native countries.
- Have them compare and contrast weather in their native countries with the cycle of seasons they are presently experiencing.
- Families can discuss expressions that are similar to the weather expressions they are learning in English. Students can then display these expressions on the bulletin board, indicating the contributor and the country of origin.
- Ask students to discuss with their families some of the weather vocabulary studied and then report back to the class on what they learned. Compare the relative paucity of words to describe "snow" in English with the wealth of terms in Russian or in some of the Eskimo languages. Lead students to discover that the weather affects culture and language.

Sharing Our Findings

- Help students make a class book listing what they have found out from their families and display it in the library to help promote global understanding.
- In class, discuss the seasons in various parts of the world, pointing out that holidays follow the rhythm of seasons. Ask students to enlist the help of their families and think of activities or types of labor that also follow the seasons.
- Ask students to work in pairs or small groups to design an ingenious way of representing such cycles. One obvious way would be to divide a circle into four quadrants, each representing one of the four basic seasons as experienced in the temperate zone. Then add circles of the same dimensions on which students and families can collaborate to map out their own particular cycle of seasons. For example, harvest time is celebrated in almost every country, along with fishing festivals,

midwinter ceremonies, etc. And while the western world has celebrated the New Year on January 1st since Roman times, many countries use different events to signal the start of the new year. In China it is based on the position of the moon; in Sierra Leone the new year starts when the rains begin; in Iran, spring signals the beginning of the new year.

CONCLUSION

This unit on Climates and Seasons demonstrates how to make use of information drawn from the varied backgrounds of your students to build interesting and useful language learning experiences. Similarly, the authentic literature from a variety of countries and cultures validates the students' sense of the importance of each person's contribution to the Global Classroom. The ideas presented here are only a beginning. By relying on your own imagination, and by encouraging students to suggest ideas for projects, you will end up with a wide variety of learning activities that are perfect for your class.

SUGGESTED READINGS

(Titles mentioned in this chapter are marked with a ♦.)

♦ Aardema, Verna. *Bringing the Rain to Kapiti Plain*. New York: Dial Books for Young Readers, 1981.

Addison-Wesley Publishing Company. *Here It's Winter.* Reading, MA, 1991.

Alexander, Ellen. *Llama and the Great Flood.* New York: Thomas Y. Crowell, 1989.

♦ Barrett, Judy. *Cloudy with a Chance of Meatballs.* New York: Macmillan, 1978.

Bendick, Jeanne. *Putting the Sun to Work.* Champaign, Illinois: Garrard Pub., 1979.

Branley, Franklyn M. *Hurricane Watch.* New York: Harper Collins, 1985.

———. *Sunshine Makes the Seasons.* New York: Thomas Y. Crowell, 1974.

Dayrell, Elphinstone. *Why the Sun and the Moon Live in the Sky.* New York: Scholastic, 1991.

De Gerez, Toni. Louhi, *Witch of North Farm.* New York: Puffin Books, 1986.

Gibbons, Gail. *The Seasons of Arnold's Apple Tree.* New York: Harcourt Brace Jovanovich, 1984.

———. *Weather Forecasting.* New York: Macmillan, 1987.

◆ Giorgiou, Constantine. *Rani, Queen of the Jungle.* Englewood Cliffs, NJ: Prentice-Hall, 1970.

◆ Gobhai, Mehlli. *Ramu and the Kite.* Englewood Cliffs, NJ: Prentice-Hall, 1986.

Greydance, Rose. *Changing Seasons—Now I Know.* Mahwah, NJ: Troll Associates, 1983.

Hader, Berta & Elmer. *The Big Snow.* New York: Macmillan, 1948.

Hague, Kathleen & Michael. *East of the Sun and West of the Moon.* New York: Harcourt Brace Jovanovich, 1980.

Jeffers, Susan. *Brother Eagle, Sister Sky.* New York: Dial Books, 1991.

Keats, Ezra Jack. *The Snowy Day.* New York: Viking Press, 1962.

Kelley, Emily. *Happy New Year.* Minneapolis, Minnesota: Carolrhoda Books, 1984.

King, Deborah. *Cloudy.* New York: Philomel Books, 1989.

Lasky, Kathryn. *Sugaring Time.* New York: Macmillan, 1983.

Lee, Jeanne. *Toad is the Uncle of Heaven,* New York: Holt, Rhinehart and Winston, 1985.

◆ Lewis, Thomas, P. *The Dragon Kite.* New York: Holt, Rhinehart and Winston, 1973.

Lindgren, Astrid. *Springtime in Noisy Village.* New York: Viking Kestrel, 1965.

◆ Matthews, Peter (ed.). *The Guinness Book of Records.* New York: Bantam Books, 1993.

Miles, Betty. *A Day of Summer.* New York: Alfred A. Knopf, 1960.

Morgan, Allen. *Sadie and the Snowman.* New York: Scholastic, 1985.

Provensen, Alice and Martin. *A Book of Seasons.* New York: Random House, 1976.

Shaw, Charles G. *It Looked Like Spilt Milk.* New York: Harper & Row, 1947.

Singer, Jane and Kurt, *Folk Tales of Mexico.* Minneapolis: T. S. Denison, 1969.

◆ Sullivan, Judith. *We Are Navajo.* New York: Harcourt Brace Jovanovich, 1976.

Van Laan, *Nancy. Rainbow Crow,* a Lenape Tale. New York: Alfred A. Knopf, 1989.

Van Straalen, Alice. *The Book of Holidays Around the World.* New York: Dutton, 1986.

◆ Wilder, Laura Ingalls. *Little House in the Big Woods.* New York: Harper & Row, 1971.

◆ ———. *Little House on the Prairie.* New York: Harper & Row, 1971.

◆ Ziefert, Harriet. *A New Coat for Anna.* New York: Alfred A. Knopf, 1986.

ADDITIONAL RESOURCES

Smallwood, Betty Ansin. *The Literature Connection: A Read-Aloud Guide for Multicultural Classrooms.* Reading, MA: Addison-Wesley, 1991. (This annotated guide to multicultural literature lists additional titles in its sections on Holidays, pages 113–121, and Seasons/Weather, pages 173–178.)

MY WEATHER CALENDAR

Name ______________________________

Sunny	Windy	Snowy	Rainy	Stormy	Cloudy

Date month/day/year	**Weather**	**Temperature** °F. or °C.	**Date** month/day/year	**Weather**	**Temperature** °F. or °C.

COMPARATIVES AND SUPERLATIVES

Name ______________________________ Date ______________

Complete the sentence with the correct form of the adjective.

Example: **Short** Eng is shorter than Josué.

dark 1. The sky is ______________ than this morning.

fast 2. Gingerbread Man was ______________ than the Fox, but Fox

smart was ______________ than Gingerbread Man.

tall 3. The redwood is ______________ than the pine.

wide 4. The Mekong River is ______________ than the Potomac.

hot 5. Yemen is ______________ than Korea.

sunny 6. It is ______________ today than yesterday.

muddy 7. Nashat's feet are ______________ than Miguel's feet.

cool 8. It is ______________ at dusk than at noon.

flat 9. The land is ______________ in Egypt than in the Cameroons.

small 10. El Salvador is the ______________ of the Central American countries.

cloudy 11. In the rainy season, the sky is ______________ than in the dry season.

scary 12. *Bunnicula* is one of the ______________ stories that we have ever read.

high 13. Mount Everest is the ______________ mountain in the world.

many 14. There are ______________ days in October than in September.

good 15. You got one of the ______________ grades on the test.

bad 16. This must be the ______________ day that I have ever had.

weird 17. The baobab has the ______________ roots that I have ever seen.

fluffy 18. This kitten has a ______________ tail than the dog.

LISSETH'S WEATHER GRAPH

Name____________________________________ Date ______________

Each morning, Lisseth and her classmates recorded the weather and temperature in their Science Logs. Please use Lisseth's weather graph of the first ten school days in January to answer the following questions in your notebook.

1/3/1994		49°F	1/10/1994		49°F
1/4/1994		58°F	1/11/1994		46°F
1/5/1994		52°F	1/12/1994		52°F
1/6/1994		46°F	1/13/1994		60°F
1/7/1994		43°F	1/14/1994		28°F

1. How many days were sunny? How many days were cloudy?
2. How many rainy days were there?
3. On which day was it stormy?
4. What was the lowest temperature? What was the highest temperature?
5. On which days was the temperature 46 degrees Fahrenheit?
6. On which days was the temperature 49 degrees Fahrenheit?
7. On which days was the temperature 52 degrees Fahrenheit?
8. On which day did the temperature go below the freezing point?
9. Compare and contrast the January temperature and weather in Lisseth's area with the weather in your area or in your country.

WHAT IS THE WEATHER LIKE?

Name________________________________ Date ______________

Place the words from the word bank in the correct column:

	Nouns	Adjectives
1.	____________	____________
2.	____________	____________
3.	____________	____________
4.	____________	____________
5.	____________	____________
6.	____________	____________
7.	____________	____________
8.	____________	____________
9.	____________	____________
10.	____________	____________

Word Bank

avalanche
breeze
breezy
brisk
cyclone
damp
drizzle
flood
fog
foggy
frost
heat
hot
humid
icy
mild
monsoon
slippery
stormy
tornado

GLOBAL WEATHER WATCH

avalanche
blowing
breezy
bright
brisk
chilly
clearing
cloudy
cold
cool
cyclone
damp
downpour
dreary
drift
drizzle
dry
dull
earthquake
eruption
flood
foggy
freezing rain
frost
gale
hail
hailstorm
hazy
heat
heat wave
hot
humid
hurricane
icy
lightning
mild
mist
monsoon
muddy
northern lights
oppressive
overcast
rainbow
rainy
rainfall
sandstorm
scorching
severe
shower
sleet
slippery
slush
snow
sprinkle
squall
stormy
sunshine
thunder
tornado
twister
typhoon
warm
wet
windy

TREES AND PLANTS
Chapter
2
OUR RICH, GREEN WORLD

CONTENT AREA LEARNING WEB

TREES AND PLANTS

SCIENCE

Nature Walk, 33, 36
Labeling parts of a tree, 34
Collecting/displaying facts about plants and trees, 35
Setting up a Nature Table/Nature Corner, 35
Comparing leaves, 37
Discussing the life cycle of an acorn, 37
Labelling plant parts, 41
Growing geraniums, 41–43
Introducing evaporation, 42
Growing seeds, 43
Observing/discussing the sunlight-growth relationship, 43, 56
Experimenting with celery, 43–44
Organizing data with charts, 47
Exploring the forest in literature, 50–51
Researching rain forests, 54
Discussing environmental benefits and hazards, 56

MATH

Taking a class poll, 43–44
Graphing, 53

LANGUAGE ARTS

Responding to questions, 37
Language experience stories, 37
Past tense, 37, 38
Irregular plurals, 37, 38, 40
Reading aloud, 37
Writing a newsletter, 38–39
Homonyms, 40
Consonant blend -tr, *40*
Root words and suffixes, 40–41
Descriptive writing, 42–43
Writing haiku poems, 52
Describing countries of origin, 53
Writing a class book, 53

SOCIAL STUDIES

Comparing foods from different countries, 37
Comparing plants from different countries, 47
Comparing books from different countries, 49–51
Planting an Arbor Day tree, 53
Documenting historical events, 54
Listing native country plant products, 56
Discussing the uses of plants around the world, 56

ART AND MUSIC

Making and using a Root Tree, 34, 52–53
Listening to nature sounds, 35
Drawing fruits and vegetables, 37
Drawing story characters, 52
Making waxed paper murals, 53

READING COMPREHENSION

Listening to stories, 36, 50
Introducing the parts of a story, 37
Story sequencing, 42
Reading for information, 44, 46, 48–49, 50
Brainstorming webs, 45
Summarizing story reactions, 47–48
Contrasting fiction/non-fiction, 48–49
Using Venn diagrams to compare stories, 49–50
Exploring myths, 51–52
Reading aloud/summarizing stories, 52, 56

FAMILY INVOLVEMENT

Sharing newsletters, 39
Making family trees, 53
Tracing native language roots, 56
Listing native country plant products, 56
Discussing the uses of plants around the world, 56
Discussing environmental benefits and hazards, 56

CHAPTER 2. TREES AND PLANTS

My father said to me,
I know the sap
that courses through the trees
as I know the blood
that flows through my veins.
We are part of the earth
and it is part of us.
The perfumed flowers are our sisters.

—CHIEF SEATTLE

Every country has its own array of trees and plants which are peculiar to that part of the world. They provide nourishment, beauty, oxygen, shelter, and protection from erosion, without which the planet could not survive.

This chapter provides many opportunities to engage the interest of the students and actively involve them in the learning process. You might start off with a Nature Walk. This activity creates an ideal situation for collaborative activities when you pair advanced level learners with beginning level students or with students from another class. For example, first and second graders can walk, observe, and talk about what they see under the watchful eyes of older students who act as their mentors. These guides can help insure the safety of their charges, and they can also point out various leaves, trees, insects, and animals discovered along the way.

The Nature Walk has more than one purpose. It helps develop the children's powers of observation. It improves their language skills. Last (but not least), it fosters a strong bond among the participants. This bond is one of the most important elements in a successful language learning experience.

A unit on trees and plants enables you to integrate language and content and to combine mathematics, science, and social studies concepts in a natural manner. Moreover, the information gathered by students in their discussions with their families can be incorporated into webs, charts, and stories as a valuable part of the collective experience. The explorations and reflections students undertake will also help instill an active respect for the environment in each of them.

SPARKING INTEREST

This section is designed to stimulate your students' interest in the world of plants and trees. It presents them with a wide range of visual, auditory, and olfactory experiences that will instill in them a desire to learn more about green growing things.

Using Visual Stimuli

A Root Tree

- A Root Tree set up in one corner of the classroom can generate a lot of excitement and can be used in many different ways: to greet new students, to record books children have read, and to show seasonal changes, to name just a few. Use the Root Tree as the focal point in a Nature Corner.

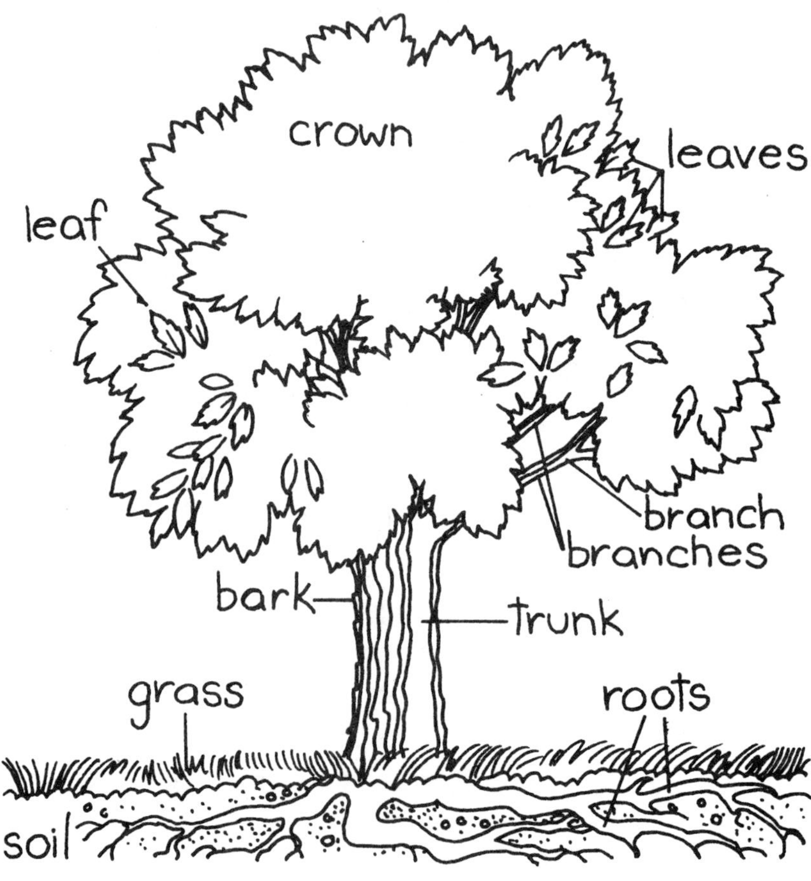

The Root Tree

MATERIALS

- ✓ *large paper to draw on*
- ✓ *colored markers or crayons*
- ✓ *string or yarn*
- ✓ *twigs, bark, and leaves*
- ✓ *magazines and catalogs with pictures of plants and trees*

- To make a Root Tree, outline a tree on a large piece of heavy paper. Include all the elements shown in the drawing above, but do not label them at this point. Display it in a prominent place in the classroom and invite students to contribute to it. They can paste on twigs, bark, and leaves. Give them pieces of coarse string of various lengths to staple to the tree to simulate roots. Discuss the parts of the tree and label them. Ask students to draw the Root Tree in their Science Learning Log and to label the parts.

- As time passes, students can write on the tree, recording key facts about plants and trees, listing the books about plants and trees they have read, etc. They can also attach to the tree pictures of interesting plants and trees they cut out of magazines. New students will immediately feel part of the group as they make their contributions to the tree. The Root Tree thus becomes a visual focus for the continuing exploration of the topic of plants and trees.

MATERIALS

✓ *nature posters*
✓ *calendars showing plants and trees*
✓ *magazines and catalogs with pictures of plants and trees*

Photographs. Put up large pictures of plants and trees on the walls of the classroom. A wide variety of commercial posters is available, but students can also have fun cutting out pictures from magazines and calendars which feature colorful photographs of plant life.

Display Books. Display books on trees and plants on an easel or a special bookshelf. Encourage students to read them individually. Suggest that small groups spend some time looking through them together and talking about what they see.

A Nature Table. Set up a Nature Table and encourage students to bring in leaves, twigs, acorns—any objects they can find that come from trees and plants. Spend some time each day talking about new additions to the nature table.

Bring the Outdoors Inside. If you have room, use an old stump as the focus of the Nature Corner. It helps bring the outdoors inside and also provides a comfortable place to sit or an interesting display surface.

Visualization. Invite students to close their eyes and visualize a favorite tree or a favorite flower from their native country. This visual experience takes place entirely in the mind's eye. Encourage them to describe to a partner what they see.

Using Auditory Stimuli

READING

✓ Under the Sunday Tree, *by Eloise Greenfield*

- Read a poem from *Under the Sunday Tree*, by Eloise Greenfield.
- Open the window on a windy day and ask students to listen to the sound of the wind in the tree branches.
- Play environmental tapes of the sounds of nature and musical tapes of songs about plants and trees.

READING
✓ The Legend of the Indian Paintbrush, *by Tomie de Paola*
✓ The Giving Tree, *by Shel Silverstein*

- Read aloud stories such as *The Legend of the Indian Paintbrush* by Tomie de Paola and *The Giving Tree* by Shel Silverstein. (Many other options are provided in the Suggested Readings section of this chapter.) *The Giving Tree* is an especially moving story about a boy and an apple tree, and students of all ages respond to it. As the story follows the boy through adolescence and into old age, the tree is always able to give the boy something to make him happy. But as the boy uses up the gifts and keeps coming back for more, we begin to wonder if the tree will have anything left to give the next time. The parallel between the tree and our dwindling natural resources is not lost on children.

Using Kinesthetic Stimuli

- Ask students to pretend to be trees. You can teach them the traditional yoga posture, or you can let students use their imaginations.

MATERIALS
✓ *paper bags*
✓ *a magnifying glass*
✓ *binoculars*

- Arrange a collaborative Nature Walk with another teacher. Give each student a recycled paper bag. Invite students to collect pine cones, bark, leaves, flowers—anything pertaining to plants and trees. Encourage them to talk about the colors, to feel the textures, and to smell each item. If possible, share a magnifying glass and a pair of binoculars to get a closer look at various tree and plant parts.

EXPANDING LANGUAGE

By now, students have had a chance to master the basic concepts and language needed to talk about plants and trees. Now you have a chance to stimulate their appetites to learn more through a variety of individual and interactive activities.

Using Students' Language Experience

- As soon as they return from their Nature Walk, students will be eager to share their treasures. Encourage all students to participate, regardless of how little or how much language they are able to use. Ask beginning level students simple questions such as: *What color is the oak leaf? Is it big? Is it little? Is the blade of grass long or short?* Intermediate level students can answer more complex questions such as: *What does the oak leaf look like? What does the maple leaf look like? What shape is the poplar leaf? What does the pine cone feel like?*

MATERIALS

✓ *"Matching Leaves" reproducible master, page 60*

- For beginning level students, use a copy of "Matching Leaves" on page 60 or make your own similar reproducible. After students have matched the leaves, you can use the pictures as the basis for a discussion of the similarities and differences among the various leaves.
- Help students create their own language experience story based on what they have seen. Write the story on the board or on large sheets of newsprint where all students can see it. This may be a good time to introduce beginning level students to some past tenses, such as *saw, found,* etc. and some irregular plural forms such as *leaves* and *branches.* If intermediate level students are ready, you might introduce the concepts of a main idea, a topic sentence, and a concluding sentence. Ask students to point out new words. Discuss them with the class. Encourage volunteers to read the story aloud.

NOTE

This activity allows you to introduce the components of a paragraph through student-generated writing.

- Show how a tiny acorn can grow up to become a rocking chair. Have students draw the main events in the life of an oak tree, from acorn to rocking chair, on a scroll. You can use shelf liner paper or recycled computer paper. Then ask them to write the story, using the third person singular and the past tense.

Building on Past Experience

MATERIALS

✓ *"Fruits and Vegetables From My Country" reproducible master, page 61*

✓ *crayons, markers, or colored pencils*

Encourage students to compare foods that are grown in the United States with those of their native countries. Make copies of "Fruits and Vegetables From My Country" on page 61 and ask students to draw pictures of plant foods common in their native lands. Beginning level students may leave the space under each picture blank, or label it in their native language. Encourage more advanced students to find out the English words from native English speakers and to fill them in.

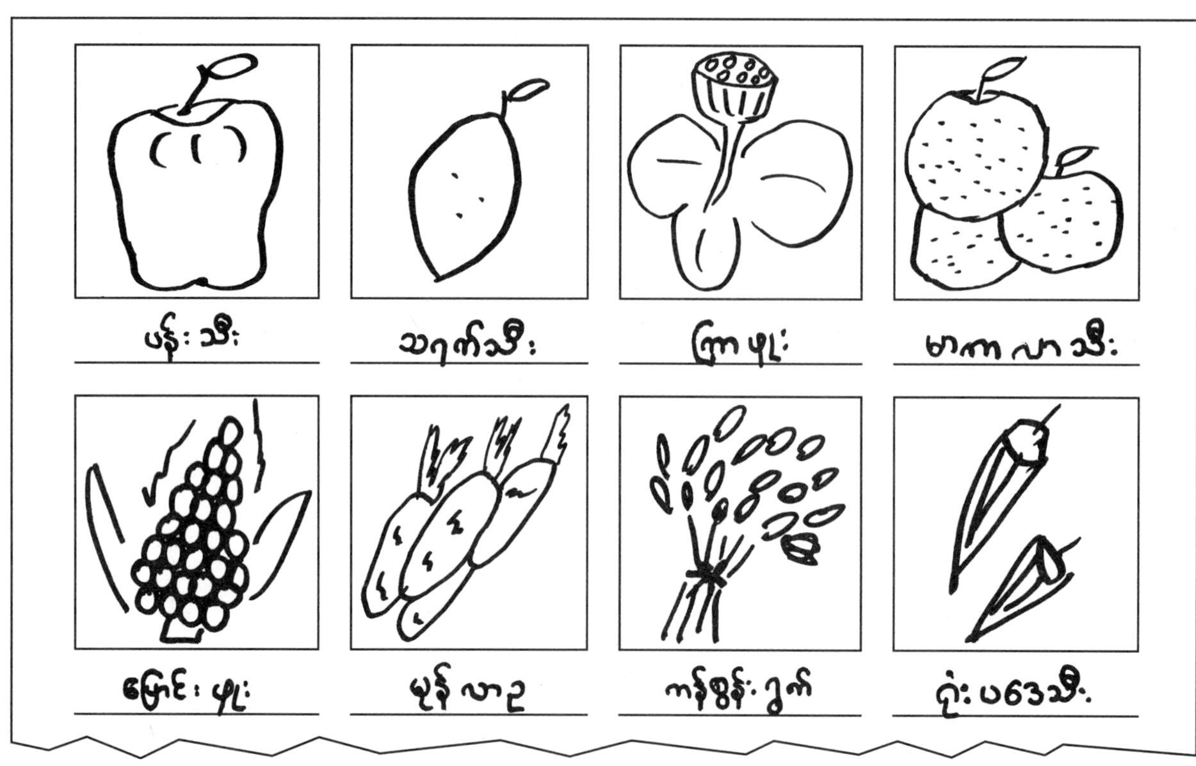

Some Fruits and Vegetables From My Country
Sonya Khin, Age 11

Writing a Newsletter

Here is another collaborative strategy which you might use to replace or augment the language experience activity above, and which can be used several times during the year.

- Divide students into groups of four or five, making sure that the groups are evenly balanced and as culturally diverse as possible. Assign one recorder per group. Give a piece of lined paper to the recorders and explain that it is their responsibility to elicit and write down a statement from each child about a Nature Walk (or other activity they have participated in together) and to collect each student's signature on the paper.
- Walk around the classroom and listen in on the process, making sure that each student contributes a news item, however small it may be. Remind the recorder to correct errors and introduce such elements as past tense markers and irregular plural forms. For example, a beginning level student might say, "I see red leaf." The recorder would write "Rosa saw red

leaves." When Rosa reads her contribution to the ESL News, she will see the correct form and practice accordingly. (The Root Tree which students created earlier will provide a catalog of plural forms not yet familiar to the beginning level student.) Encourage recorders to sound out words they do not know and circle them if they are not sure how to spell them. Provide a word list of plant words as a reference.

- When each group has completed its section, collect the papers and compile the individual contributions into a single newsletter. If possible, prepare a version of the newsletter on a computer. Print copies for each student and post a copy on the classroom wall. Individual newsletters provide good reading and language reinforcement and can be discussed at home with students' families, whose language may very well be enriched, too.

Nature Walk

Stacy found a pine cone. It is brown and light and prickly.

Monica found a piece of bark. It feels rough.

Lisseth found yellow, green, and brown leaves and two acorns.

Juan found a big, greenish leaf with pointed edges.

Hugo says that if you lie down on pine needles, they will tickle you.

Picnic

On Saturday there was a picnic down by the

A Newsletter Article

Looking at Vocabulary and Spelling

MATERIALS
✓ social studies books and trade books
✓ large paper for a wall chart
✓ markers or crayons

Two-faced Words. Illustrate the concept of homonyms using the words *trunk, bark,* and *fall.* Then brainstorm with students a list of ten tree and plant words which have more than one meaning. (These may include *chop, board, plant, stick, crown, top,* and *spring.*) Post the list on the wall along with a listing of the two meanings for each word. Ask students to illustrate the two meanings of each word and to write a sentence for each in their notebooks.

Irregular Plurals. Using *branch/branches, bush/bushes,* and *leaf/leaves* as examples, you might incorporate a lesson on irregular plurals in this unit. Other examples might include *cherry/cherries, berry/berries,* and *mango/mangoes.* Later, divide the class into several groups, assigning each one a particular type of irregular plural (for example, *f/ves* or *y/ies).* Ask each group to list as many examples as possible of this type of plural.

***The Consonant Blend* tr.** A unit on trees is an appropriate time to introduce or review the consonant blend *tr.* Brainstorm with students and provide pictures of *tr* words, such as *traffic, trail,* and *trade.* Advanced students in upper grade levels might study the prefix *trans* at this time. Invite them to go through trade books and social studies books and find words beginning with *trans.* Discuss the meaning or each word and post a list of ten words for further study. These might include *transfer, transform, translate, translator, translation, transmit,* etc.

Roots and Suffixes

MATERIALS
✓ filled-in Science Learning Logs
✓ notebooks
✓ construction paper
✓ posterboard

- Use the Root Tree for a lesson on root words and suffixes. Print twenty to thirty words gleaned from the children's Science Learning Logs and writings on the board. Use these as the basis for a lesson on suffixes (or "word endings", if the term *suffix* seems too advanced). As a follow-up, have students copy the words in their notebooks, remove the suffixes, and identify the root words. Once they have finished, ask them to take turns writing the correct root words on the board. Then give each student a chance to write a few words containing suffixes on colored leaves of their choice, while they write the root of each word on a thin strip of posterboard.

Students will enjoy sticking their leaves on the crown of the tree, while you staple the root words to the roots of the tree.

MATERIALS

✓ "Find the Roots" reproducible master, 62

- Make copies of "Find the Roots" on page 62 and distribute them to all students. Go over the instructions and have students complete the activity as pair work in class, or individually for homework. Instead of using the reproducible in this book, you may wish to prepare a similar one featuring words that students have been using in class.
- Once the suffix activity is completed, you can review with students the rules they applied. For example, they may have had to double the final consonant before adding the suffix.

Growing Geraniums

MATERIALS

✓ geranium plants
✓ glass jars or plastic containers
✓ watering can
✓ ruler
✓ masking tape
✓ Science Learning Logs

I have grown geraniums in my classroom over the years because geraniums flourish in the local area and because each fall my old geraniums provide enough cuttings for my 25 second and third graders. We also grow spider plants, impatiens, and others, but none has been as popular as the bright red flowered geraniums. Of course, you should feel free to experiment with any plant that grows well in your local area.

Preparation and Materials. You'll need one or two geraniums from the previous season and some small jars or clear plastic containers to grow the plants in. Supply rulers and a small watering can. Use masking tape to attach the students' names to each plant.

Procedures

- Day One. Explain to students that they will learn how to have a "green thumb" and that they will record the changes in their geranium each day. Bring in your geranium and explain that most plants need to be trimmed and that this is also a way to grow healthy new plants. Cut back the stalks that are too long, snipping right above a leaf. Give one cutting to each student. Have students place the cuttings in jars, fill the jars with water, and then draw pictures of the cuttings in their Science Learning Logs.
- Day Two. Draw a geranium on the board. Point out the most important parts, such as *roots, stem, leaves,* and *flowers.*

Then ask students to use their Science Learning Logs to label their plants and to record what they have done so far.

- Day Three. Have students count the number of leaves on their geraniums and record it in their Science Learning Logs. A student might write, *My geranium has five green leaves. It has two big leaves. It has three small leaves. It has no flowers.*
- Day Four. Have students add water to their jars and measure the water level. They can then observe their plants and practice using numbers to talk about them. Start them off with questions such as: *How many big leaves are there? How many flowers are there? How many inches of water are there in yours?*
- Day Five. Repeat some of the previous activities. The routine may seem repetitious, but students are eagerly awaiting the day when the first root appears, and they are acquiring good language and observation skills in the process. Discuss each change with them and share in their enthusiasm. The excitement comes to a climax when one lucky student first spots a tiny root emerging from the stem of a geranium. Everyone should record the important date.

  Monday, October 15th, 1994
  Soe-Hae's geranium has one root.

MATERIALS

✓ *aluminum pan*
✓ *geranium clipping with sturdy roots*
✓ *pots for plants*
✓ *potting soil*

Making a Science Connection. While carrying out the geranium activity, ask students to measure carefully the water level and calculate how much it falls each day. Ask them what the difference is between the two levels. Then ask them to try to explain where they think the water went. Introduce and explain the word *evaporation.* Place some water in an aluminum pan and check the level the next day. Then discuss where it went. After each geranium has grown sturdy roots, bring in soil, distribute small pots, and invite students to plant their geraniums and take them home.

Sorting out the Sequence. As a follow-up activity, write instructions for growing geraniums, recording each step of the process on a separate strip of paper. Mix them up and ask students to place them in the correct sequence.

Matching Sentences with Pictures. Make copies of "Azadeh's Geranium" on page 63 and distribute them to beginning and

MATERIALS
- ✓ "Azadeh's Geranium" reproducible master, page 63
- ✓ scissors
- ✓ paste
- ✓ plain paper

intermediate level students. Have them cut out the pictures and the sentence strips, match each sentence with a picture, and paste the matched sets in the correct order on another sheet of paper.

Writing "How to" Instructions. Students with stronger language skills might also be able to use this lesson on growing geraniums as an opportunity to practice writing "how to" instructions.

Growing Marigold or Bean Seeds

This activity has a dual purpose: to teach students that plants grow from seeds, and to demonstrate that plants need sunlight to survive. Use discarded starter pots, peat moss pots, or empty egg cartons. Explain to students the importance of well-drained soil and put shards of old clay pots or small pebbles at the bottom of the pots.

MATERIALS
- ✓ marigold or bean seeds
- ✓ egg cartons
- ✓ small pebbles
- ✓ masking tape and a marker or pen
- ✓ potting soil
- ✓ small trowel or spoon
- ✓ ruler
- ✓ Science Learning Logs

- Invite all students to participate in the planting process. Ask each student to label a pot, using a marker and masking tape. Have them fill the bottom of the pot with soil, using a small trowel or an old spoon, and use a pencil to poke a hole into the soil. Then have them measure the hole, which should be two inches deep, and place three or four seeds in it. Show them how to cover the seeds with soil and water the seeds.
- Place the plants in the sun, on a windowsill if possible. Have students water plants lightly every day and record the growth in their Science Learning Logs as they did with the geranium.
- If possible, and if this is not too heart-breaking for the students, conduct a second experiment in which you attempt to grow plants in a windowless room. These plants will obviously die. Ask students to predict the outcome ahead of time. Take a poll and post the results. Compare the plants in the sun with those in the dark on a daily basis. When the experiment is completed, elicit the observation that plants need light to grow.

Experimenting with Celery

- Bring in a few stalks of fresh celery. Ask students what they know about celery. Place it in a jar or bottle containing water and label it. Add a few drops of food coloring to the water. Ask students what they think will happen. Write down their predictions on a large sheet of paper and put it up on the wall.

- Then cut some other celery stalks into small pieces and have a tasting party. Discuss the opposites *raw* and *cooked.* Take a poll to find out how many students like raw celery and how many don't. Discuss which other vegetables can be eaten raw. Brainstorm a list and put it up on the wall.
- The next day, talk about the coloring process of the celery and compare the students' predictions with the results. Ask students to enter all the data in their Science Learning Logs.

MATERIALS

- ✓ *some stalks of celery*
- ✓ *glass jar or bottle*
- ✓ *food coloring*
- ✓ *large paper for wall chart*
- ✓ *markers*
- ✓ *Science Learning Logs*

READING AND REFLECTING

As we are becoming increasingly concerned about the environment and wonder whether trees will continue to grow and grace our children's world, the number of publications on this topic keeps on expanding. This makes it relatively easy to provide students with a choice of books and a mine of information to dig from.

A unit on trees and plants provides a golden opportunity for collecting data, teaching research skills, and stressing the distinction between realistic writing and fanciful stories—between non-fiction and fiction. We'll start with activities based on non-fiction works. Later, we will contrast the use of fiction with the use of non-fiction works.

Using Non-Fiction

Activities for Beginning Level Students

- A reading from a basal or a trade book might be used either as a starting point or as a validation of student observations.
- Such books as *A Tree Is Nice*, by Janice Udry, and *A Tree Is a Plant,* by Clyde Robert Bulla, which can be used in science with first and second graders, are written in simple language and provide beginning level students with a lot of information. After reading and discussing these books with the class,

READING

- ✓ A Tree Is Nice, *by Janice Udry*
- ✓ A Tree Is a Plant, *by Clyde Robert Bulla*
- ✓ *Science Learning Logs*

ask students to record what they have learned in their Science Learning Logs.

- As prereading activities, invite students to work in pairs or small groups and make a list of all the objects made out of wood or derived from wood which they can see in the classroom. After the noisy hunt is over, ask students to share and compare their lists. Compile their contributions into a huge web which may include a piñata, wooden toys made out of birch, or writing paper made out of the bark of the daphne tree which grows in Nepal. The web below will give you an idea of how to set up your web. As we will see in the Getting Families Involved section of this chapter, this list can be expanded at home, making use of input from family members. As students read, they should be encouraged to add to the list.

NOTE

Brainstorming sessions like these and the resulting webs serve as "What do you know?" activities. They generate a considerable amount of vocabulary and a great deal of creative thinking on the part of students at all ability levels. The webs also serve as springboards for discussions of such linguistic elements as phonics, consonant blends, irregular plurals, etc.

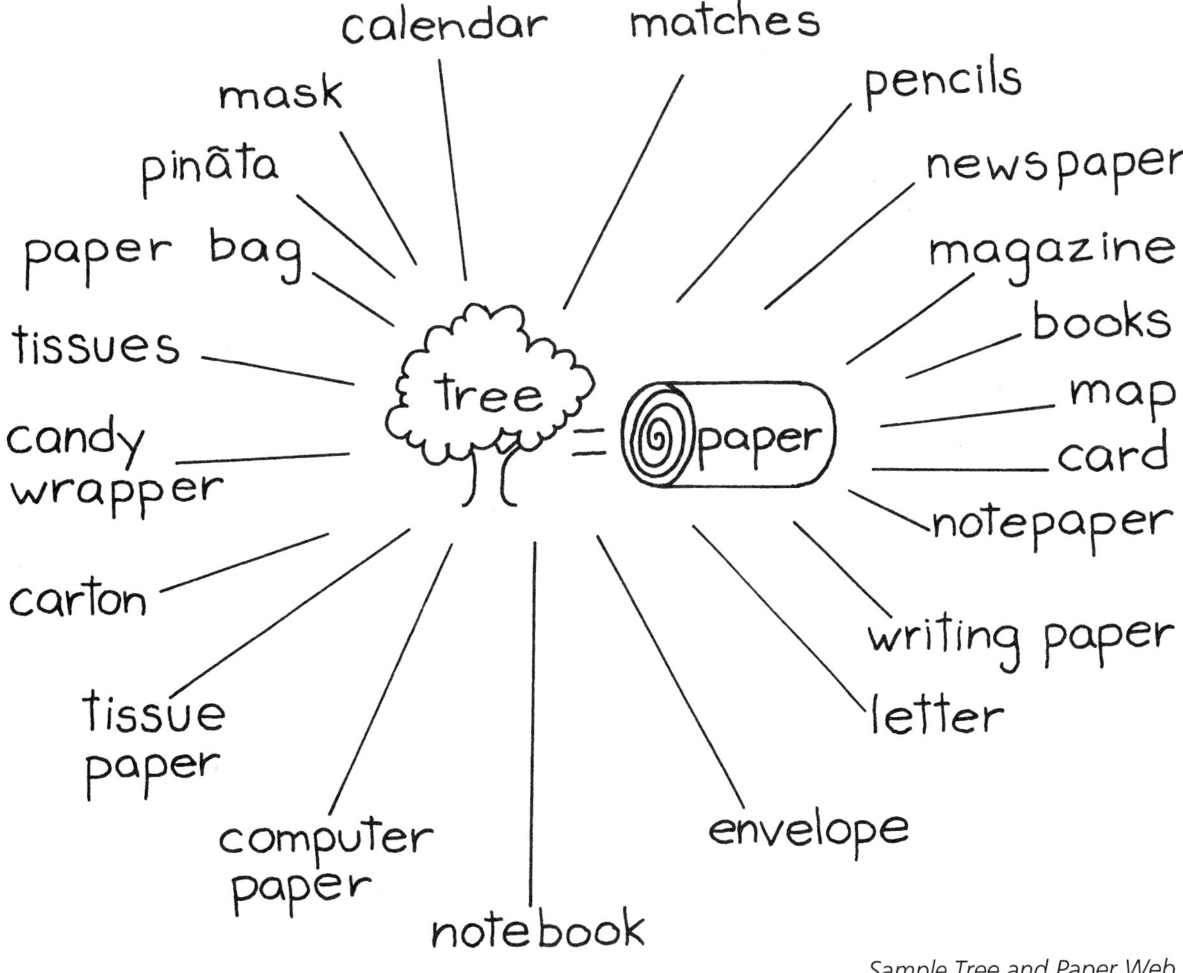

Sample Tree and Paper Web

READING

✓ From Tree to Table, *by Ali Mitgusch (or a chapter from a basal textbook that describes the lumbering process)*

- Read *From Tree to Table,* by Ali Mitgusch, or choose a chapter from a basal textbook that describes the lumbering process. Provide students with strips of recycled paper and ask them to draw pictures of what happened to the tree. Encourage students to write simple sentences describing the pictures.

Activities for Intermediate and Advanced Level Students

- More advanced students can benefit from the use of similar webbing activities focusing on more specialized concepts such as occupations and the tools needed to perform each one. Another semantic mapping activity might focus on words that are used to describe wood, or the various forms that wood takes on. The webs below are examples of the latter two types.

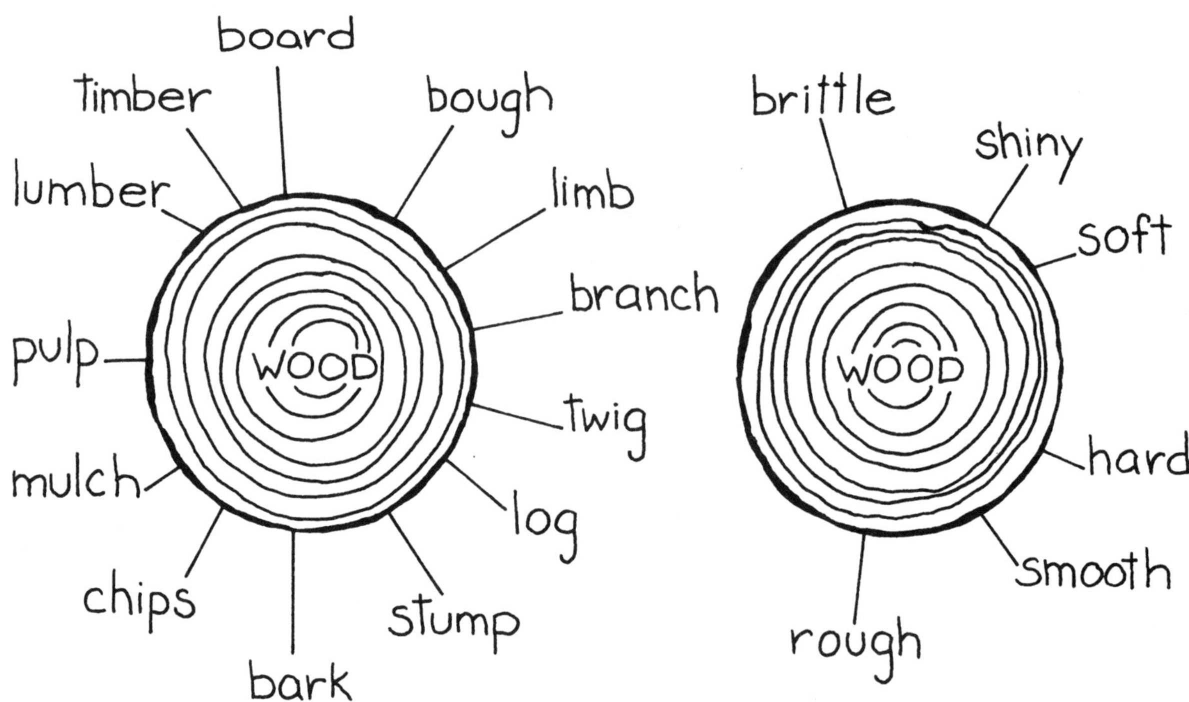

Semantic Maps Related to Wood

- Show students how to use charts to collect and analyze data they encounter in their reading. Since charts constitute excellent frameworks for organizing information, you can ask students to categorize facts in their notebooks in charts like the one that follows. Encourage beginning level students to use simple drawings as column heads. More advanced students may be ready to use the terms *deciduous* and *coniferous.*

Three Types of Trees

TREES WITH LEAVES	TREES WITH NEEDLES	PALMS
lose leaves in the fall	stay green all year round — have green needles	have big, long, narrow leaves
maple, oak, aspen	fir, pine	royal palm, date palm cabbage palmetto

- Another type of chart uses as headings the countries your students are particularly interested in. Invite students to list and locate the plants and trees they encounter in their reading. Use this list as a springboard for collecting data and doing further research on trees, how they impact our daily lives, and how they affect the environment.

What Trees Grow Here?

BRAZIL	CAMBODIA	INDIA	FRANCE
ferns	banana trees	neem	lime
rubber trees	bamboo	fig	poplar
canopy trees	tamarind tree	mango	chestnut

Using Fiction

Book Response assignments provide an exciting way for students to share their delight in a particular book with the rest of the class. The example that follows shows how one student chose to summarize her reaction to a book called *Miss Rumphius* both in print and in the form of a drawing.

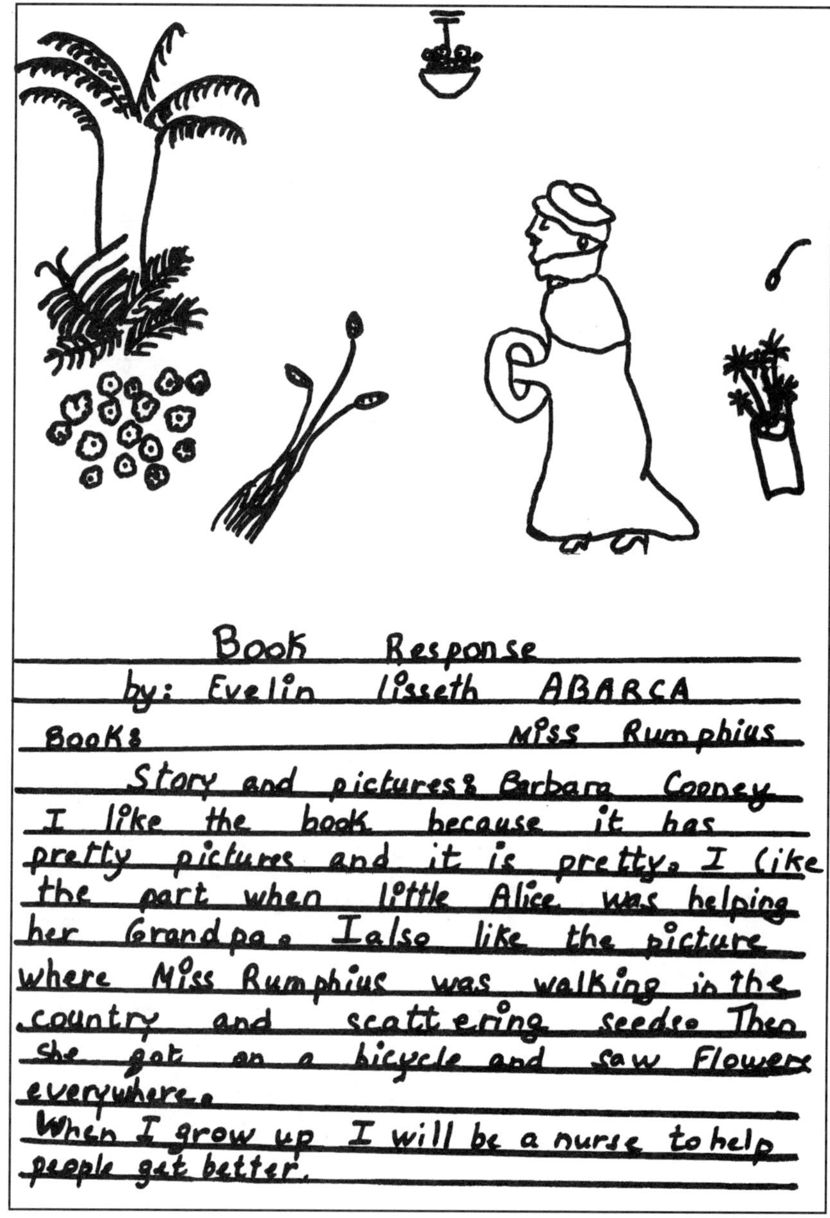

Miss Rumphius
Evelin Lisseth Abarca, Age 10

Contrasting Fiction and Non-Fiction

The following are examples of books which provide useful fiction/non-fiction contrasts. You will undoubtedly find others which offer similar opportunities.

- Since many rain forest trees may grow up to 120 feet tall (as high as a 15-story building), it may be a good idea to discuss

✓ Rain Forest Secrets, *by Arthur Dorros*

READING

the book *Rain Forest Secrets,* by Arthur Dorros, at length. Emphasize that all the information in the book is factual. At the same time, bear in mind that a number of students may come from cultures where the supernatural often coexists with the real, where "phi" (Lao spirits) and ghosts abound and play tricks on people, and where Neil Armstrong's historic landing on the moon belongs to the realm of the imaginary.

✓ Jack and the Beanstalk *(any version)*

✓ Taro and the Bamboo Shoot, *by Masako Matsumo*

READING

- After studying *Rain Forest Secrets,* contrast it with the story of *Jack and the Beanstalk,* which may already be familiar to a majority of students, or read *Taro and the Bamboo Shoot,* a folktale by Masako Matsumo. This Japanese story describes the adventure of a nine-year old boy, Taro, who lived in a small village, completely cut off from the rest of the world. In both tales, the plant or tree was chopped down, and both boys became rich. Jack and his mother never had to worry about money again, thanks to the giant's gold. Likewise, Taro and his mother, uncles, aunts, and indeed, the whole village, enjoyed the products from the sea, which they added to their diet of bamboo for well-balanced meals.
- This study in contrasts can include all three books. Point out that although both folktales offer happy endings, the sad truth about deforestation is that each time a tree is chopped down, the world loses a valuable resource.

Using A Venn Diagram

- A Venn diagram like the one below is a useful way of analyzing, contrasting, and summarizing information about two different stories. The material that applies to each story individually is placed in the left side of the left-hand circle and the right side of the right-hand circle. Material that applies to both stories is placed in the central, overlapping portion of the two circles. Ask students to use colored chalk to fill in facts on a blank diagram you outline on the board. They can then see clearly the similarities and differences between the stories.
- You can also create three-circle Venn diagrams to compare and contrast elements of three different stories. Show the elements which apply to only one of the stories in the part of

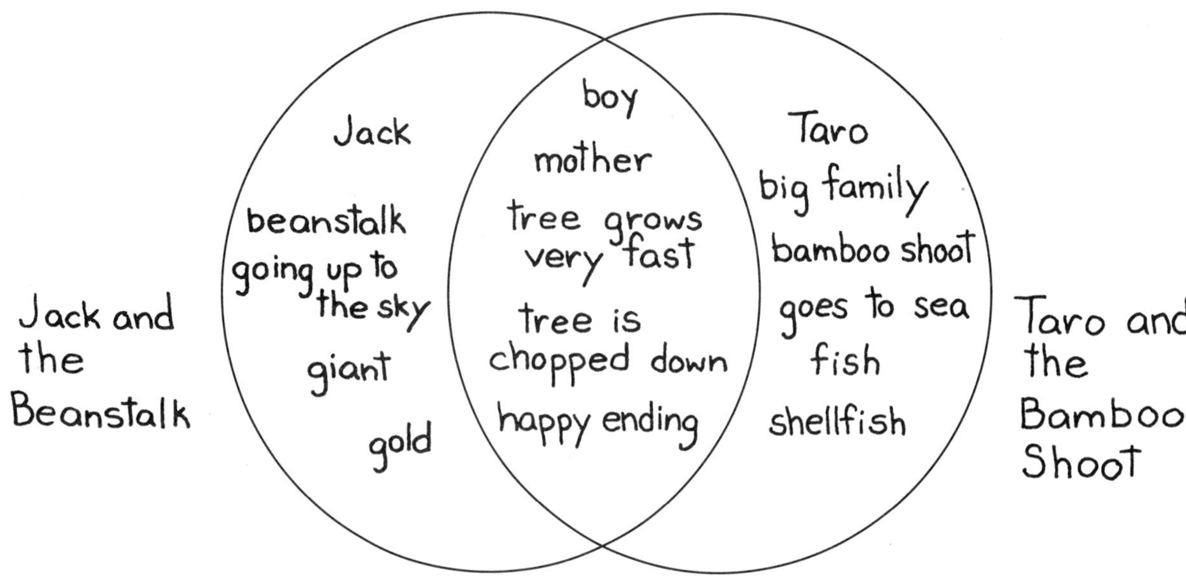

A Venn Diagram Contrasting Two Stories

each circle that doesn't intersect with the other circles. Elements shared by two stories appear in the places where two circles overlap, and elements shared by all three stories are placed in the central area where all three circles overlap.

Exploring the Forest

- Take some time to emphasize the place of the forest in literature. Although the examples of *Little Red Riding Hood* and Prokofiev's *Peter and the Wolf* immediately come to mind, I refrain from using them, since they depict the Wolf as a villain. Instead, select stories which show the forest as a refuge for birds, mammals, and other animals which live there and depend upon its resources for food, homes, and nests. Read out loud to students, building up the suspense and emphasizing the feeling of mystery.
- If it is available, read *The Legend of El Dorado* by Beatriz Vidal. Let them discover the moon-shaped Lake Guatavita surrounded by the forest, a mysterious, unknown territory which contrasts so strongly with the security of the village.
- Continue the study of forest literature by reading, discussing, comparing, and contrasting books from several other countries.

READING
✓ The Legend of El Dorado, *by Beatriz Vidal*

✓ Ntombi's Song, *by Jenny Seed*
✓ The Magic Ringlet, *by Konstantin Paustovskii*

READING

You might choose *Ntombi's Song* by Jenny Seed, and *The Magic Ringlet* by Konstantin Paustovskii. In *Ntombi's Song,* the forest looms as a dark, dense, threatening place inhabited by the monster ISIQUQUMADEVU. A perfect contrast to this book is *The Magic Ringlet,* the story of yet another brave little girl, Varyusha, on a journey through the snowy pine forest to help her ailing grandfather. Ask students to draw a line down the middle of a piece of paper and make side-by-side illustrations showing their impressions of these contrasting forests.

✓ Atariba and Niguayona, *by Harriet Rohmer and Jesus Guerrero Rea*

READING

- In *Atariba and Niguayona,* by Harriet Rohmer and Jesus Guerrero Rea, the young Niguayona despairs as he sees his childhood playmate, Atariba, languish in her hammock, afflicted with a disease that even the "bohique," or healer, is unable to cure. One day, a messenger from the gods flies in disguised as a macaw and tells Niguayona that the fruit of the caimoni tree can cure Atariba. Niguayona immediately sets out on his quest through the forest, alive with tree frogs, owls, and macaws. Brainstorm with students a list of stories in which a forest animal brings an important message to a human in distress.
- After reading each story, make a list of the trees, birds, animals, and other forest elements encountered in each. Discuss the vegetation and climate and their impact on the story. Discuss the art work and the soft whites of *The Magic Ringlet,* as contrasted with the vivid yellows, reds, purples, blacks, and greens that illustrate the Puerto Rican legend of *Atariba and Niguayona.* Then ask students to compare one of these stories with a story about trees or forests that they may have read or heard in their native countries. Invite students to share their stories with the rest of the class.

Exploring Myths

As you wind up the reading and research in this unit, talk about the special status held by trees in myths and various cultures. According to the Bushman's theory of the Creation, as related in *When Hippo Was Hairy and Other Tales from Africa* by Nick Greaves, the earth and plants came first, followed by the animals.

READING

✓ When Hippo Was Hairy and Other Tales from Africa, *by Nick Greaves*

✓ The King and the Mangoes, *a Jataka tale*

✓ The Parrot and the Fig Tree, *a Jataka tale*

✓ Brother Eagle, Sister Sky, *by Susan Jeffers*

Man came last. In other stories, trees are the givers of life (or play important roles) as in two Jataka tales, *The King and the Mangoes* (a tale my Lao students are especially fond of) and *The Parrot and the Fig Tree.* Since Native American culture is so intricately connected to the land, the trees, and nature, you might like to end this section with Chief Seattle's message, as retold in Susan Jeffers's magnificent book *Brother Eagle, Sister Sky.*

- Divide the class into four groups and have each group read one of the stories. As the groups work together, move around the room monitoring progress and answering any questions students may have. Then ask each group to make a poster showing the main character(s) at a crucial point in their story. Later, ask each group to summarize their story and share their drawing with the class.

CREATING AND SHARING

By now your classroom has already come alive with charts, pictures, webs, and a trunkful of information. Graphic representations not only add color to the walls, they also hold the students' interest, optimize learning, and help develop intellectual skills.

The Root Tree

Record the Changing Seasons

MATERIALS

✓ *the Root Tree, prepared earlier*

✓ *yellow and pink tissue paper*

✓ *construction paper*

- The preparation of the Root Tree was described at the beginning of the chapter. One way to use the Root Tree is to record the changing of the seasons in some symbolic form. In the spring, ask students to decorate it with buds or blossoms of yellow and pink tissue paper.
- Then teach them how to write Japanese-style haiku poems about spring. These poems have three lines of five, then seven, then five syllables. Post these poems on the wall around the tree. In the summer add leaves made from green construction paper and use yellow, brown, and orange leaves in the fall.

Welcome New Students. The Root Tree can also be used to welcome new students to your classroom. Depending upon the tree and your local area, just write their names on apples, oranges, or mangoes cut out of construction paper and hang them on the tree.

Collect Favorite Poems. You can create a "Poet-tree" by hanging the students' favorite poems on the branches.

Make a Family Tree. Some students may want to make a family tree. They can pin the names of family members to the trunk and branches of the tree to show others in the class a simple genealogy. You may have to teach the names of various relations such as *brother-in-law* to beginning level students.

Enrichment Activities

Activities for Beginning and Intermediate Level Students

MATERIALS
- ✓ *leaves collected on the Nature Walk*
- ✓ *waxed paper*
- ✓ *construction paper for frames*
- ✓ *crayons or markers*

- Use leaves collected on your Nature Walk to make waxed paper murals. Press the leaves between two sheets of waxed paper. Give students construction paper frames for the leaves, and ask them to use crayons to decorate the frames with illustrations showing the current season. They can then display these colorful reminders of their Nature Walk.
- After the walk, make a list of all the trees that students identified. Make a graph showing how many people discovered each tree and display it on the wall.

MATERIALS
- ✓ *a young tree large enough to plant outdoors*
- ✓ *shovel*

- On Arbor Day, June 14th, plant a tree with your students. A local nursery may be willing to provide a tree without charge. If possible, get the nurseryman to talk to your class about how to plant the tree and what they should do to be sure the tree continues to thrive.

Writing Activities

MATERIALS
- ✓ *"Trees and Plants" reproducible master, page 64*

- Encourage students to close their eyes and pretend to shoot a movie of themselves in their native country or area. What trees do they see in the background? Have them write short descriptions telling which ones were their favorites and why.
- Compile the stories and pictures of trees into a class book. Use a copy of "Trees and Plants" on page 64 as a cover, or design one of your own.

✓ *Rain Forest Secrets, by Arthur Dorros*

READING

Research Work

- To introduce a research and writing project, read *Rain Forest Secrets,* written and illustrated by Arthur Dorros. Ask students to locate rain forests on a world map or a globe. Ask questions about rain forests such as: *What is a rain forest? Where are tropical rain forests located? What is the temperature like in a rain forest? How much rain do rain forests get? Where is the largest rain forest in the world? How fast are rain forests disappearing?*
- Then ask students to brainstorm and make a list of research topics focused on the rain forest. Assign a deadline and let students work in small groups or pairs to complete the project.

Presentations. Have some of the more advanced students write up their research and present what they have learned in the form of essays, pictures, videos, graphs, or in any other audio or visual manner they wish.

Culminating Activity

Help students key the history of mankind to the annual rings of a tree. Use the illustration on page 55 as a guide. This project allows all students to feel involved and all cultures to be recognized for their legacies to mankind.

- First ask students to draw a series of 27 concentric rings, which will represent the stump of a 2,700-year-old redwood tree. They should use a large piece of heavy paper (butcher's paper works fine), wasting as little paper as possible. Explain that each ring will represent one century.
- Then ask them to go through some social studies books and record all the peaceful events that have affected mankind since the tree was just a seed. Each student may want to concentrate on events from his or her country of origin.
- Cut large leaves out of construction paper and use them to record the events. You can color code the leaves and use them to represent various types of events such as scientific discoveries, geographic discoveries, and the completion of works of art.

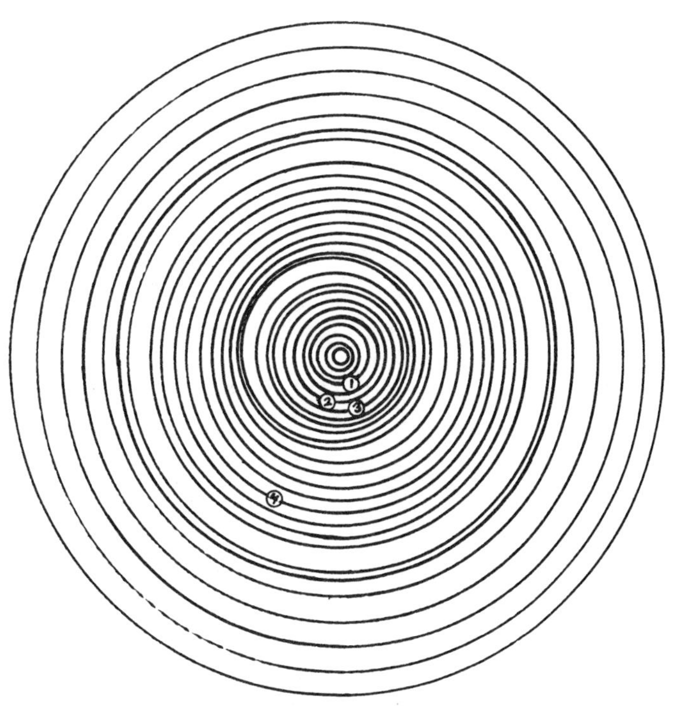

① 500 B.C. Age of city-state of Athens
② 300 B.C. Temple of the Sun built in Teotihuacan, México
③ 200 B.C. Great Wall of China built
④ 1000 A.D. Vikings land in America

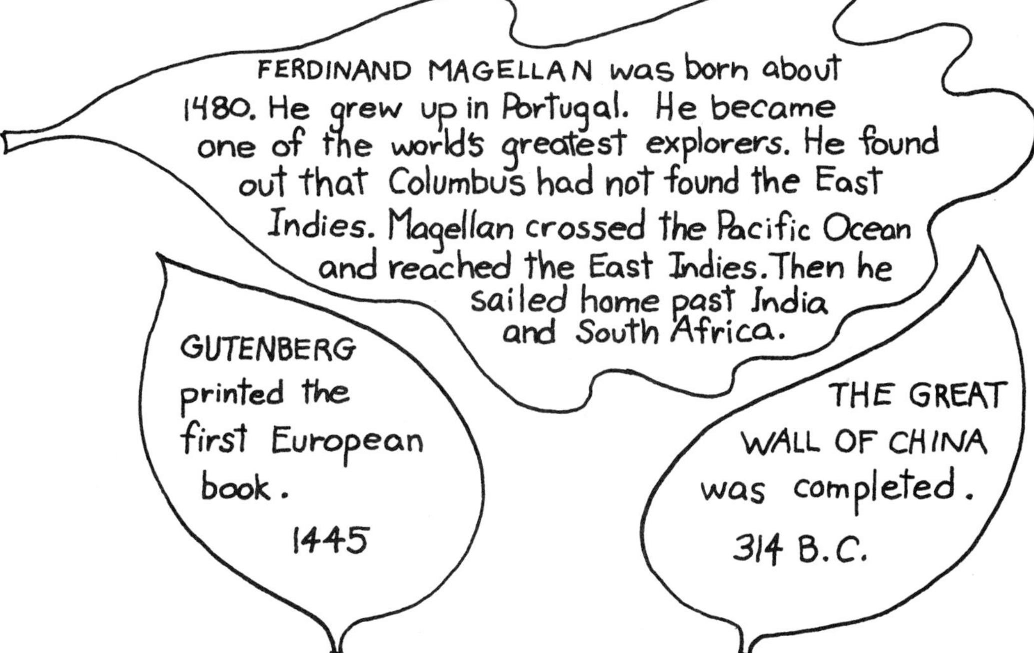

In the rings of a tree, the history of mankind.

GETTING FAMILIES INVOLVED

A unit on trees and plants provides a variety of topics for students to talk with their families about. Students may:

- ask their families to help them trace the roots of their languages. Students can then contribute to a collective Root Tree diagram showing how their language fits in to the overall pattern of world languages.
- get help in compiling a list of trees native to their countries and discussing with their families the impact of weather and climate on the vegetation.
- ask their families to help them complete a list of various tree products that come from their native countries. For example, cork from Spain and Portugal, latex from the rubber trees of Vietnam and Malaysia, and oranges from the trees of Mexico.
- work with their families in compiling a list of the various ways in which trees are used around the world. For example, half the trees in Nepal are used for firewood, and banana leaves are used as plates in Laos and as umbrellas in India.
- discuss with family members the problems caused by deforestation in countries such as Brazil, Nepal, and Yugoslavia. These talks can also touch on the resulting erosion, flooding (Bangladesh), and desertification (the Sahara) that follow deforestation.
- reflect on the effects of pollution and acid rain in the northeastern part of the United States and the Black Forest in Germany.
- give examples of the healing powers of trees and plants. For example, in India the usefulness of the neem tree was recognized in Sanskrit writings. Nowadays, it is well-known for preventing insect infestation. Herb teas (for example, yerba buena, camomile, and Linden Blüten) are used worldwide to treat a multitude of mild ailments.
- retell a story about a specific tree or group of trees.
- brainstorm a list of ways to help save the environment.

CONCLUSION

A unit on trees and plants lends itself well to all kinds of activities. It enables teachers, students, and family members to become enthusiastic participants in the instruction process. It opens the door for units on animal life, food, and clothing, as it points out the interdependence of all things, living and non-living.

SUGGESTED READINGS

(Titles mentioned in this chapter are marked with a ◆.)

Addison-Wesley Publishing Company. *The Farmer and the Beet.* Reading, MA, 1989.

Adoff, Arnold. *Flamboyan.* New York: Harcourt Brace Jovanovich, 1983. (Parents' Choice Award 1983 and National Council of Teachers of English Award for Poetry for Children)

Althea. *Leaves from Trees*. Cambridge, England: Dinosaur Publications, 1981.

Bailey, Donna. *Facts About Forests.* Austin, Texas: Steck-Vaughn, 1990.

Beame, Rona. *Leaf and Tree Guide*. New York: Workman Publishing, 1989.

Bourgeois, Paulette. *The Amazing Paper Book*. Reading, Massachusetts: Addison-Wesley Publishing Company, 1989.

◆ Bulla, Clyde Robert. *A Tree Is a Plant*. New York: Thomas Y. Crowell, 1960.

Cooney, Barbara. *Miss Rumphius*. New York: Viking Penguin, 1982. (Winner of the American Book Award)

◆ de Paola, Tomie. *The Legend of the Indian Paintbrush.* New York: Scholastic, 1988.

◆ Dorros, Arthur. *Rain Forest Secrets*. New York: Scholastic, 1990.

Ehlert, Lois. *Planting a Rainbow*. New York: Harcourt Brace Jovanovich, 1988.

George, Jean. *The Hole in the Tree.* New York: Dutton, 1957.

- Greaves, Nick. *When Hippo Was Hairy and Other Tales from Africa*. New York: Barron's, 1988.
- Greenfield, Eloise. *Under the Sunday Tree.* New York: Harper Trophy, 1991.

Hawkinson, John. *The Old Stump*. Chicago: Albert Whitman & Co., 1965.

Ingoglia, Gina. *Look Inside a Tree*. New York: Grosset & Dunlap, 1991.

- Jataka Tales. *The King and the Mangoes*. Emeryville, California: Dharma Publishing, 1975.
- ———. *The Parrot and the Fig Tree*. Oakland, California: Dharma Publishing, 1991, 1975.
- Jeffers, Susan. *Brother Eagle, Sister Sky.* New York: Dial Books, 1991.

Jordan, Helene J. *Seeds by Wind and Water.* New York: Crowell, 1962.

Lasky, Kathryn. *Sugaring Time*. New York: Macmillan, 1983. (A Newbery Honor Book)

Markmann, Erika. *Grow It! An Indoor/Outdoor Gardening Guide for Kids.* New York: Random House, 1991.

- Matsumo, Masako. *Taro and the Bamboo Shoot*. New York: Pantheon Books, 1964.
- Mitgusch, Ali. *From Tree to Table*. Minneapolis, Minnesota: Carolrhoda Books, 1981.

Orgel, Doris. *Cindy's Sad and Happy Tree*. New York: Alfred A. Knopf, 1967.

- Paustovskii, Konstantin. *The Magic Ringlet*. Reading, Massachusetts: Addison-Wesley, 1971.

Rockwell, Robert E., et al. *Hug a Tree & Other Things to Do Outdoors with Young Children.* Mt. Rainier, Maryland: Gryphon House, Inc., 1983.

- Rohmer, Harriet et al. *Atariba and Niguayona*. San Francisco: Children's Book Press, 1988.
- Seed, Jenny. *Ntombi's Song.* Boston: Beacon Press, 1987.

Selsam, Millicent E. et al. *A First Look at Leaves.* New York: Walker & Co., 1972.

Siberell, Anne. *a journey to paradise.* New York: Henry Holt & Co., 1990.

- Silverstein, Shel. *The Giving Tree.* New York: Harper & Row, 1964.

Turner, Ann. *Heron Street*. New York: Scholastic, 1989.

- Udry, Janice May. *A Tree Is Nice*. New York: Harper Trophy, 1987. (Winner of the Caldecott Medal)

Vidal, Beatriz. *The Legend of El Dorado.* New York: Alfred A. Knopf, 1991.

Vorhees, Duance and Mueller, Mark. *The Woodcutter and the Heavenly Maiden.* Elizabeth, New Jersey: Hollym Corporation, 1990.

Watts, May Theilgaard. *Flower Finder*. Berkeley, California: Nature Study Guide Publishers, 1955.

———. *Tree Finder*. Berkeley, California: Nature Study Guide Publishers, 1963.

———. *Winter Tree Finder*. Berkeley, California: Nature Study Guide Publishers, 1970.

MATCHING LEAVES

Name____ Date ________________

Find the matching leaves on the left and right sides of the page. Color the matching leaves the same color.

FRUITS AND VEGETABLES FROM MY COUNTRY

Name____________________ Date __________

FIND THE ROOTS

Name________________________________ Date ______________

The leaves are falling off this tree. Find the root words and write them by the roots of the tree.

climbing
hopping
greener
sunny
highest
walked
taller
cloudier
wooden
windy

AZADEH'S GERANIUM

Name______________________________ Date ______________

Azadeh wants to grow a geranium at home for her cousin Shagi. Help her put the instructions in the right order.

Put the geranium on the window sill.
Cover with soil.
Put soil in a clay pot.
Make a hole in the middle and plant the cutting.
Water the soil.

TREES AND PLANTS

ANIMALS AROUND THE WORLD
Chapter
3
TAME, WILD, OR MYTHICAL

CONTENT AREA LEARNING WEB

ANIMALS AROUND THE WORLD

SCIENCE

Displaying animal pictures, 68

Showing animal filmstrips, 68

Nature Walk, 68

Studying animal behaviors/characteristics, 70, 72

Studying endangered species, 81, 83

LANGUAGE ARTS

Studying similarities and differences, 69, 80, 86, 87

Classifying animals, 70

Comparatives and superlatives, 71, 73

Developing animal vocabulary, 72–75, 77, 80

Synonyms, 72

Animal booklets, 84–85

Writing riddles, 85

Homonyms, 86

ART AND MUSIC

Animal songs and sounds, 68, 72, 87

Imitating animal movements, 68

Drawing animal pictures, 69, 72

Drawing story scenes, 77

Making magic fans, 77–78

Making animal masks, 82

Building dioramas, 82

Animal pop-up books, 82

Making mobiles, 82

Stuffed toy animals, 83

Word pictures 83

Animal sculptures, 83

Animal riddle booklets, 85

Animal jigsaw puzzles, 86

Life-size animal art, 86–87

SOCIAL STUDIES

Visiting a farm or zoo, 69

Listing and comparing animals in many countries, 73–74

Comparing cultures, 77, 79–80, 88

Community clean-up campaign, 84

Promoting recycling activities, 84

READING COMPREHENSION

Reading for information, 74–76

Listening to stories, 76–77, 79–80

Retelling/summarizing a story, 76, 79

Introducing fables, 77

Contrasting folktales, 79–80

Using Venn diagrams to compare stories, 80

MATH

Measuring activities, 70–71, 87

Comparing U.S. and metric measurements, 71

Proportions, 87

FAMILY INVOLVEMENT

Learning native language animal sounds, 87

Learning native country songs and dances, 87

Learning native country proverbs, 88

CHAPTER 3. ANIMALS AROUND THE WORLD

> The world grows smaller and smaller, and more and more interdependent... Today, more than ever before, life must be characterized by a sense of universal responsibility, not only nation-to-nation and human-to-human, but also human to other forms of life.
>
> —His Holiness the Fourteenth Dalaï Lama of Tibet

Children are instinctively curious about animals, be they domesticated, wild, or mythical. Since animals constitute a favorite topic among children around the world, they provide a golden opportunity for vocabulary development and language expansion activities.

Before embarking on this unit, ask your librarian to put aside for your use as many books about animals as possible. Visit the local used bookstore, borrow books from friends, and collect old or current issues of nature magazines, such as *Ranger Rick, Your Big Backyard, National Wildlife,* etc. Hang posters on the walls and display Big Books and regular books in a Book Corner in order to arouse the children's curiosity. A colorful poster depicting the diversity of nature, a folktale from a distant land, or the awesome sight of Canadian geese flying in formation overhead may be the catalyst for the launch of this unit.

Encourage students to browse through the books and magazines. Explain to them that each student will become an "expert" on an animal of their choice, and that he or she will then teach the rest of the class what they have learned about that animal.

SPARKING INTEREST

This section contains a listing of activities that you can use to help motivate your students to learn more about animals. This list is just a beginning, however. Use it as a springboard as you think about ways of appealing to your students' keen senses of sight, sound, hearing, smell, and touch.

Using Visual Stimuli

- Glue a group of animal postcards on posterboard and display it on the bulletin board.

MATERIALS

✓ *postcards, posters, and other photographs of animals along with posterboard, scissors, and paste*

✓ *magazines featuring animal pictures*

✓ *drawing paper and colored markers*

✓ *filmstrips about animals*

- A wide variety of animal posters is available commercially, but students will enjoy drawing their own on large sheets of paper.
- Students can cut up old magazines and make animal collages. Suggest that they make a collage featuring as many examples of one type of animal (for example, monkeys) as they can.
- Show a filmstrip about animals without using the sound track. Encourage students to say anything they wish about the animals shown.

Using Auditory Stimuli

MATERIALS

✓ *audio tapes of animal sounds*

- Sing songs about animals and their activities.
- Play audio tapes of animal sounds.
- Ask individual students to take turns making animal sounds as the rest of the class guesses what animal it is. Start with easy ones like the meow of a cat or the bark of a dog. Then encourage students to make the sounds of less common animals from their native countries. They might imitate the water buffalo, which is found in Laos, or the lion, which lives in Africa.

Using Kinesthetic Stimuli

READING

✓ Another Here and Now Storybook *by Lucy Sprague Mitchell*

- Have students imitate the movements of various animals. You can inspire children by reading Evelyn Beyer's poem *Jump or Jiggle,* found in Lucy Sprague Mitchell's *Another Here and Now Storybook.*
- Open the classroom window and observe the birds, squirrels, cats, dogs, or any other animals that are running or flying around outside.
- Take a Nature Walk. A short walk near the school is a good start. If possible take students to a place that will have a richer and more varied array of wildlife, such as a field, a pond, or a stretch of conservation land. Bring a camera to take pictures. Encourage students to talk with each other about what they are seeing and to make sketches of any animal that particularly interests them.

MATERIALS

✓ Animals From My Country" *reproducible master, page 93*

- Visit a farm or a petting zoo where students can touch and smell the animals as well as see them. Encourage them to list all the different textures of skin, fur, and feathers they are able to touch.
- Ask students to draw pictures of animals from their native countries. Make copies of "Animals From My Country" on page 93 and distribute them to all students. If they wish, students can label the animals using native language or English words. Here is a sample from one of my students.

Animals From My Country
Sung-Won Yi, Age 13

EXPANDING LANGUAGE

At this point, students' have had a chance to see, hear, smell, touch, and talk about a variety of animals. Here are some ideas that allow students to build on what they already know as they interact with each other while doing whole-class, group, and paired activities.

Using Charts to Classify Information

- Place a wide variety of animal pictures where all students can see them and ask them to find the similarities and differences among what the various animals can do. You can help out beginning level students by pantomiming the verbs, such as *hop, fly,* and *swim.* Then point to the picture of a designated

MATERIALS
- ✓ *large pictures of a wide variety of animals*
- ✓ *"Things Animals Can Do" reproducible master, page 94*

animal and ask questions such as *Can a rabbit hop? Can a bee fly?* Then have students place the animal pictures in three different stacks: the fliers, the hoppers, the swimmers.

NOTE
The word can *is used in this exercise to avoid requiring beginning students to produce the third person singular* s *in the present tense.*

- Expand the activity to include questions about which animals can run and which animals can live on land. Make copies of "Things Animals Can Do" on page 94 and distribute them to all students or put the headings on the board and have students make their own charts. Then have them classify each animal you have discussed under one or more headings.

MATERIALS
- ✓ *small pictures of animals*
- ✓ *cardboard*
- ✓ *scissors*
- ✓ *paste*
- ✓ *"Things Animals Have" reproducible master, page 95*

- Make animal cards by pasting pictures of various animals onto cardboard squares. Give each student a card. Have students practice saying the names of all the animals, introducing any words for them. Then ask the students to give you back the cards in certain categories. For example, you might say, *Please give me all the animals that have tails.* Follow up this activity by having students fill out another chart. Make copies of "Things Animals Have" on page 95 and distribute them to all students. Ask students either to cut out small pictures of animals and paste them in the correct column of the following chart, or to draw their own pictures on the chart.
- More advanced students can make their own charts and classify animals according to these categories: *fur, feathers, scales,* and *hide.*
- Later on some students may be able to classify animals under these headings: *amphibians, birds, fish, insects, mammals,* and *reptiles.*

Using a Measuring Strip

MATERIALS
- ✓ *butcher paper*
- ✓ *masking tape*
- ✓ *laminating materials*

This activity allows you to integrate mathematics into this unit and is a great source of excitement and wonder for students. It is also an excellent springboard for teaching the comparative and superlative.

- Cut a ten-foot-long piece of butcher paper in two lengthwise. Join the two pieces together with masking tape to form a twenty-foot-long measuring strip.
- Ask each student to choose a different animal and use a picture dictionary or encyclopedia to find out the length of the

animal. Mark the measurement on the measuring strip with a marker.

- Later, remove the masking tape and laminate the two strips side-by-side (in order to save laminating paper). After laminating, cut them apart again lengthwise and rejoin them (end-to-end) with strong masking tape. You will find that this gigantic ruler is a much-used fixture in the classroom.

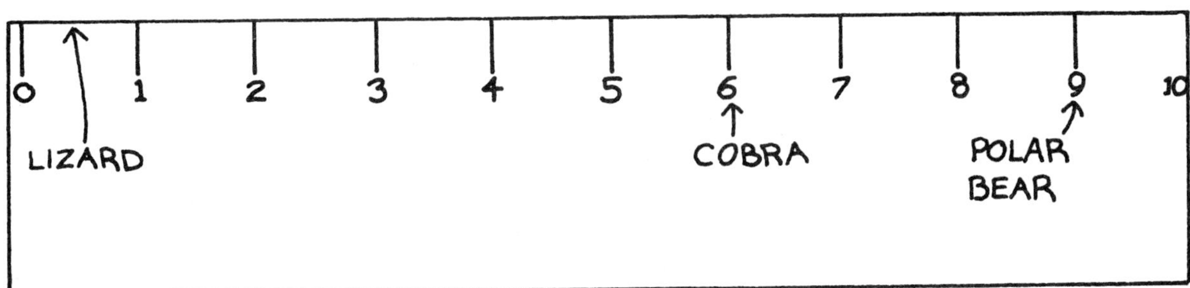

Measuring Strip (marked in feet)

- A similar strip may be created and used to measure the heights of various animals.
- Measuring strips like these can also be used:
  - to compare inches and feet to centimeters and meters.
  - to review equivalences, such as 1 foot = 12 inches and 1 yard = 3 feet.
  - to write math problems. Students may work in groups of two or three. For example:

    Sung-Won's tiger is 5½ feet high at the shoulder.
    Jennifer's llama is 4½ feet high at the shoulder.
    How much taller is Sung-Won's tiger?

  - to write sentences, using comparative and superlative forms. For example:

    John's monkey is taller than Sonya's jackrabbit.
    Elena's elk is bigger than Hugo's gray fox.

MATERIALS

✓ *"Comparatives and Superlatives" reproducible master, page 96*

- Many students will now be ready to take a quiz on comparatives and superlatives. Make copies of "Comparatives and Superlatives" on page 96 and distribute them to students who can benefit from this activity.

Enrichment Activities

These activities can be done by individuals, in pairs, or in small groups. Tailor your assignments to the needs and abilities of your particular students.

- Ask students to draw an animal. Have them label the paws, claws, tail, trunk, horns or any other significant part. Then ask students to compare and contrast the parts of the animal they have drawn with similar parts of the human body.

The Parts of an Animal
Evelin Abarca, age 10

- Ask students to list the names of animals and what their young are called. For example, cats have kittens, dogs have puppies, and does have fawns.
- Have students list animals and the sounds they make. Beginning students may imitate the sounds these animals make. More advanced students may be able to provide the correct verb for the sound.
- Have students make a chart of sizes like the one that follows. First brainstorm with the class a list of synonyms for *small* and *big.* Classify them according to size. Then make a large chart of these terms and post it on the wall as a source of new vocabulary to use during class discussions and writing.

Chart of Sizes

✓ The Guinness Book of Records, *edited by Peter Matthews*

READING

- Play The Superlative Game. Enlist the help of your librarian in rounding up as many copies of *The Guinness Book of Records* as you can. Have students work in pairs or individually. Write a list of ten questions on the board. For example, *What is the heaviest mammal in the world?* Students must answer questions in complete sentences. The student (or students) with the most correct facts and complete sentences wins.

Using Charts for Comparison and Contrast

You can create a variety of other chart formats which will help your students expand what they know about animals. The following sample headings will give you ideas for making up charts which fit the needs and ability levels of your particular class.

- A simple chart can be made to contrast the kinds of animals that live in the United States with those that live in other countries.

United States	Other Countries
mountain lion	toucan (Brazil)
	koala (Australia)

- A more complex chart can be used to gather information about the animals in countries around the world.

  Cambodia | Korea | Laos | Liberia | Nicaragua

- A further refinement of the previous chart can be used to classify animals according to the continent on which they are found.

  Africa | Asia | Europe | North America | South America

READING AND REFLECTING

At this point, all of the basic vocabulary about animals has been introduced and developed, and the basic concepts have been presented. Students are now prepared to begin reading and locating answers to specific questions. The type of books you choose and the level of difficulty must, of course, be tailored to the needs and ability levels of your students.

Using Webs with Non-Fiction Readings

Webs are often used to help prepare children to read a chosen book. Through this activity, they have a chance to discuss the categories of information and create lists of specific words that may appear in the reading. All students have a chance to contribute their ideas to (and ask questions about) the web on the board. This activity is very flexible and can be adapted for use with a variety of ability levels.

Two sample webs on animals follow. The first one shows the type of information you might elicit from beginning level students. The second shows what you might get from a group of more advanced students. (For a quick review of how to conduct a webbing activity, refer back to Chapter Two, page 45 for a description of how the class put together a tree and paper web.)

Researching Animal Rights

After completing the second web, ask students to describe any domestic animals they own or have seen in their neighborhoods.

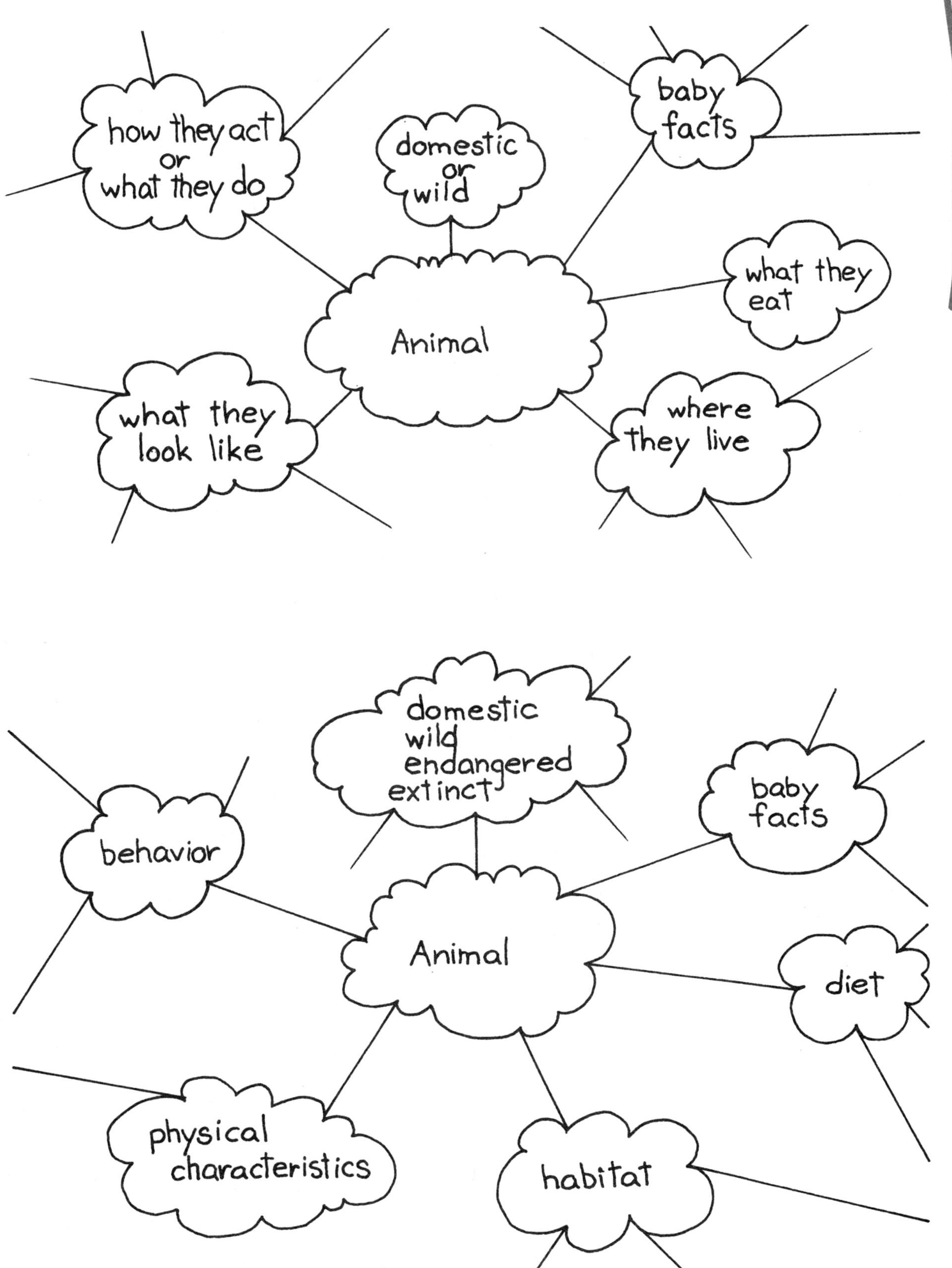

Two Sample Webs on Animals

✓ The Animal Rights Handbook, Everyday Ways To Save Animal Lives, *by the ASPCA*

READING

Then talk about how those animals are treated. Ask students if they know how to go about helping an animal they see being mistreated. Place the ASPCA book, *The Animal Rights Handbook, Everyday Ways To Save Animal Lives,* in the Reading Corner so that it will be available to all students. Ask each student to find out one way they can help protect one kind of animal from mistreatment. Encourage groups of students to collaborate on making animal rights posters to display around the school building.

Using Fiction

When the research is over, you might want to switch from non-fiction to fiction for a change of pace. I have several favorite stories which I like to use again and again. You will undoubtedly develop your own list of favorites.

✓ The Story of Ferdinand, *by Munro Leaf*

READING

- Lower grade students like *The Story of Ferdinand,* by Munro Leaf. It's about a peaceful bull who much prefers sitting in the shade of a cork tree and smelling the flowers to fighting in the arena. When you read the book you will enjoy not only the story and its humorous ending, but also Robert Lawson's marvelous ink drawings, some of which are reminiscent of scenes from *Don Quixote*. After reading the book, you might ask students to tell their own versions of a story in which an animal (perhaps their pet) does not behave the way people expect it to.
- My students always enjoy *The Fox and the Rooster,* a pop-up book in Russian which I bought years ago in Moscow for my own children. This story proved to me that books do not necessarily have to be in English to be useful. I asked Stacy, a Russian second-grader who arrived at the beginning of the school year, to show the pictures and read the story—in Russian, of course—to my other second and third graders. Nobody grumbled about not understanding. Stacy asked leading questions, provided clues, and guided her peers into grasping the main points of the story. *Then, and only then,* did she translate the book, which very much appealed to the rest of the class. Some students decided to rewrite this Russian tale in which, once more, Fox lives up to his reputation

as a rather undesirable neighbor. You may know of other non-English books that students will find just as appealing.

✓ Three Aesop Fox Fables, *by Paul Galdone* — READING

- Aesop depicts the fox in the same unflattering light in *The Fox and the Grapes,* and *The Fox and the Stork.* However, in *The Fox and the Crow,* the fox outwits the crow by using flattery. Paul Galdone's *Three Aesop Fox Fables* would be a good choice for introducing students to these fables. After reading the stories, ask students which one they like best, and why. Then have them choose their favorite scene from their favorite story and make a drawing including the main characters and showing the setting. Ask students to share their work with the rest of the class.

✓ One Fine Day, *by Nonny Hogrogian* — READING

- A good fox story to end with is *One Fine Day*, by Nonny Hogrogian. This humorous Armenian folktale tells about yet another crafty fox, but this one is rehabilitated by the end of the story. The amusing repetition of phrases and the charming drawings delight children's ears and eyes.

Using an Art Activity as a Follow-Up

✓ Badger and the Magic Fan, *by Tony Johnston* — READING

- *Badger and the Magic Fan,* by Tony Johnston, is an engaging trickster tale from Japan. A greedy badger seizes an opportunity to whisk away a magic fan from several goblin children by causing them to quarrel. He plays havoc as he uses the stolen fan's power to make noses grow longer and shorter. In the end, he becomes the victim of the fan's magic as his own long nose becomes a post in a bridge in the clouds. The story delights children, and the illustrations (by Tomie dePaola) can serve as a jumping-off-point for cross-cultural comparisons of food, clothing, and shelter.
- An activity in which students make magic fans is an excellent follow-up to this story. A two-sided fan can also be a useful vehicle for reinforcing vocabulary words or grammar points which can be categorized into two dissimilar groups. Students write or paste words from each group on opposite sides of the fan. Past and present tenses, related nouns and verbs, sky words and ground words, light things and heavy things, and proper nouns and common nouns are just a few of the groupings which might provide a bridge to other parts of

MATERIALS
- ✓ *construction paper*
- ✓ *markers*
- ✓ *scissors*
- ✓ *chopsticks*
- ✓ *stapler*

your curriculum. You can laminate your own reusable chart-size fan for reuse and/or have the children make individual fans, following these simple steps.

- Step One. Fold a piece of 12-by-18-inch paper in half widthwise.
- Step Two. Draw as large an oval as you can on the folded paper, letting about three inches of the oval run off the folded side.
- Step Three. Cut out the double oval (keeping the folded edge at the top) and allow children to decorate or illustrate each side.
- Step Four. Unfold the fan and attach a stick (chopsticks are good and cheap if you can get them) with several strips of masking tape to the middle of one side.
- Step Five. Fold the other side down and staple the two sides together at several points around the edges.

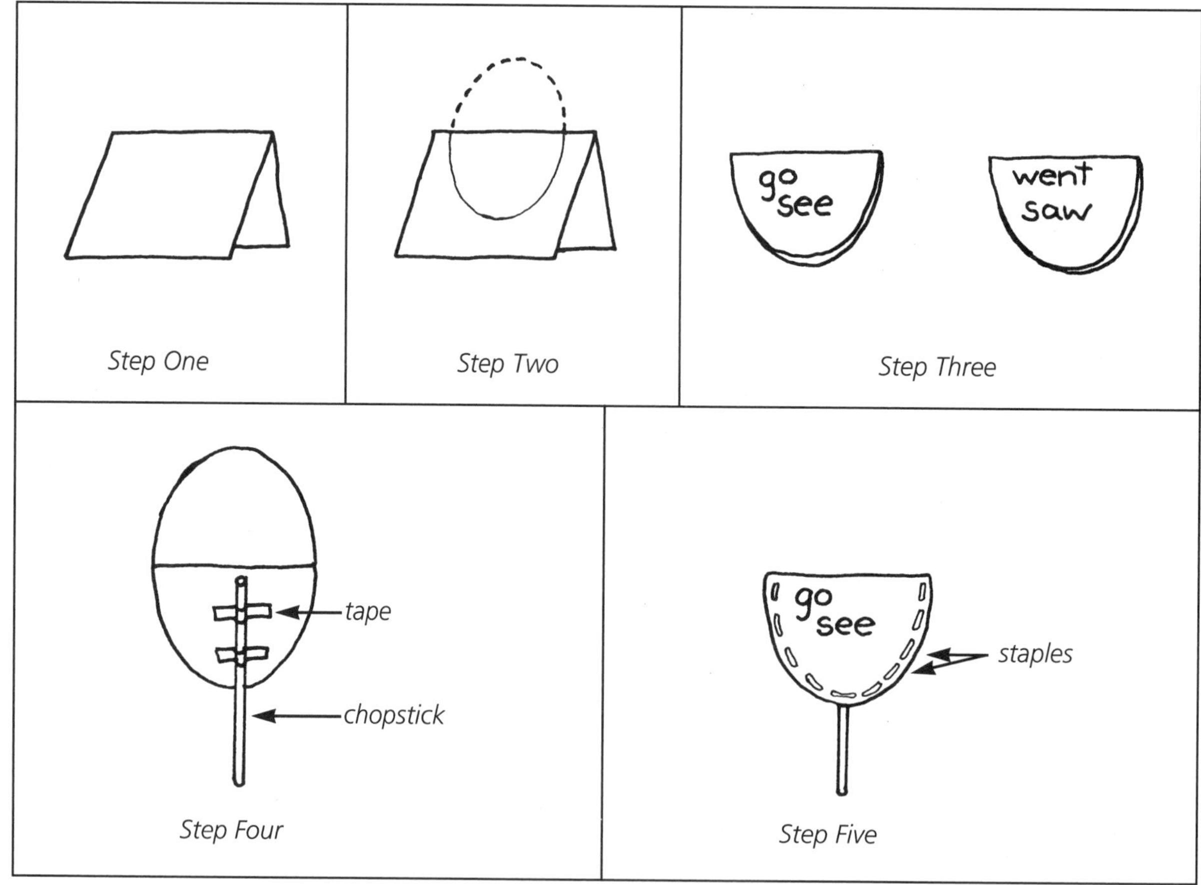

Using Multicultural Folktales

The object of reading these multicultural tales is to provide enjoyment to our students, to enrich their lives, to increase their vocabulary, to develop their thinking skills, to draw parallels between stories, and to emphasize pride in each student's own cultural heritage. Often you will marvel at the perceptiveness of your young charges when they point out details you might not have noticed. For example, one of my students discovered that the anthropomorphic features in *Nine-In-One, Grr! Grr!* were similar to those in *Llama and the Great Flood,* an Andean folktale by Ellen Alexander. It sometimes takes a child's eye to discern faces in rocks and mountains and I am sometimes so intent upon the meaning of the story that I miss important elements hidden in the pictures.

One exciting thing about living and teaching in this day and age is that we have access to more multicultural literature than ever before. The titles I have used are not necessarily those you will use. With a little effort you will be able to develop your own lists and your own systems.

✓ Nine-In-One, Grr! Grr!, *by Blia Xiong*

READING

- *Nine-In-One, Grr! Grr!* told by Blia Xiong and adapted by Cathy Spagnoli, is a folktale from the Hmong people of Laos which can be read to students of all ages and all proficiency levels. It explains how the eu bird, a clever black bird, fooled Tiger. Nancy Hom's illustrations of the peaceful, benevolent female tiger, the angular, aggressive black bird, and the embroidery which adorns the clothes of the great Shao (a sort of shaman) and his wife, are lovely as well as accurate in detail. Ask students to summarize how the eu bird tricked Tiger into having fewer babies than she planned. Then relate the story to the concept of overpopulation and how it can cause the extinction of a species.

✓ Judge Rabbit and the Tree Spirit, *by Lina Mao Wall*

READING

- At this point you might introduce another folktale, this time one from Cambodia called *Judge Rabbit and the Tree Spirit.* This is a bilingual folktale in Khmer and in English told by Lina Mao Wall and adapted by Cathy Spagnoli. It concerns a mischievous tree spirit who plays havoc with human beings. You might want to first have your students brainstorm a list of ways they think a tree spirit might play tricks on humans, and then compare what students think with what actually happens in the story. This book is interesting in many ways. First of all, it is a Cambodian folktale, with Khmer writing on the same page as the illustration, so that the delicate characters (which are borrowed from the Sanskrit) appear as an extension of the art work. Secondly, the book presents yet another facet of a very popular animal, the rabbit, and grants it human-like qualities. Judge Rabbit is not at all like Beatrix Potter's frolicking, mischievous Peter.

READING
✓ The Tortoise and the Hare, *(any version)*

- Ask students to compare the rabbit who competes with the tortoise in the fable *The Tortoise and the Hare* (and looks rather foolish at the end), with the rabbit in *Judge Rabbit and the Tree Spirit.* This meek but self-assured figure helps human beings in times of need, and shares his wisdom with them. Ask students to tell about folktales from their countries in which there are animals which resemble one of the rabbits they have read about. Take this opportunity to have students brainstorm a list of abstract adjectives describing some of the more prevalent personality characteristics found in human beings and often attributed to animals.

Using Venn Diagrams

READING
✓ The Mitten, a Ukrainian Folktale, *by Jan Brett*
✓ The Old Man's Mitten, *by Yvonne Pollock*

A Venn diagram like the one that follows is a useful way of comparing information from two different animal stories. The material that applies to each story individually is placed in the left side of the left-hand circle and the right side of the right-hand circle. Material that applies to both stories is placed in the central, overlapping portion of the two circles. Students can then discuss the stories, their similarities, and their differences.

Choosing Relevant Readings

There are so many books one could choose from that it is often difficult to make final choices. Basals, be they old or new, should not be ignored. In them you can find stories about working elephants and camels, seeing-eye dogs, and other revered animals. Once you have helped open their minds, students will come to you, eager to share their new books with you.

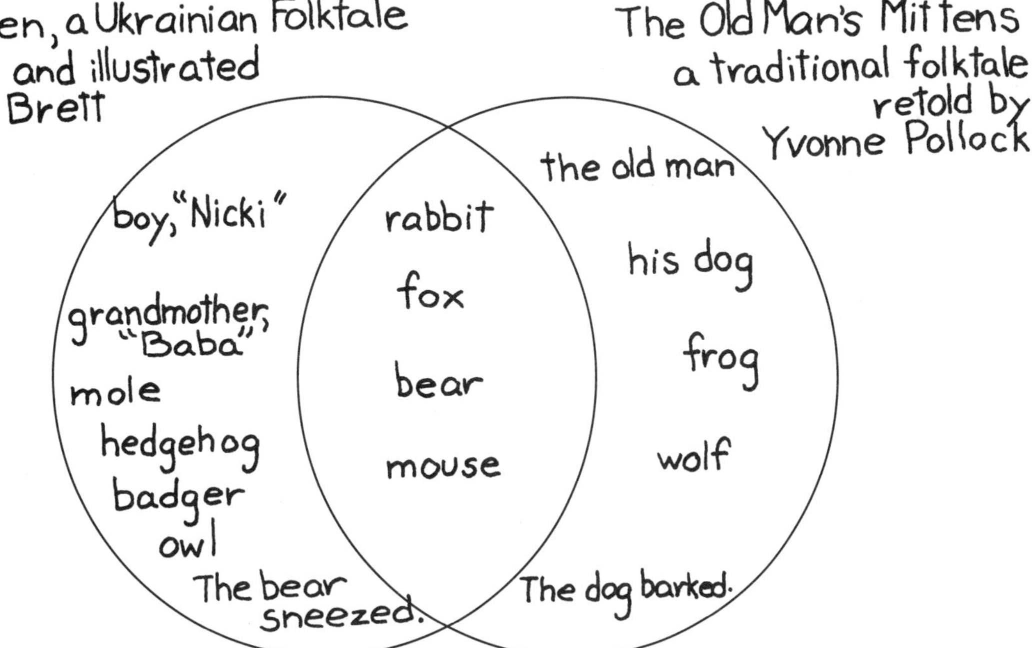

Children's concern about endangered species can serve as a strong motivation for further reading about animals. Discuss with the class which species appear to be on the way to extinction and make a list on the board. Ask students to read at least one book or one article about an endangered animal of their choice and prepare to tell the class about it. Suggest that they bring the book or magazine to class and show pictures of their animal when they give their presentation.

✓ The Land I Lost, *by Quang Nhuon Huynh*

READING

Students are also motivated to read books that relate to their own past (or present) experiences. One book that taught me how a single story can make a big difference in a student's life is *The Land I Lost,* by Quang Nhuon Huynh. This book describes life in a small hamlet in the central highlands of Vietnam. The animal encounters described by the author include helping tame water buffalo, capturing fish caught by otters, and watching the attack of a horse snake. One of my semi-literate students from Vietnam used to beg me to read him the boy's adventures over and over. Even though his verbal and reading skills were limited, this sixth-grader gained a great deal of vocabulary, language, and enjoyment from my reading of this book.

The Land I Lost motivated him to record his own thoughts and experiences in a journal. His language sometimes lacked conventional syntax, but it was always full of narrative power. Obviously, the reason the book worked so well is that he could identify with the author since he, too, came from the same region of Vietnam. The match-up is not always as obvious as this. However, finding the right book for the right child is always a key element in facilitating the emotional as well as the linguistic adjustment of our students.

CREATING AND SHARING

The topic of animals is one which all students respond to, regardless of age, sex, or national background. This chapter is full of opportunities for you to use animal topics as a way to motivate students to use their new language in the creation of original stories, posters, games, and charts. You can guide your students through some of the projects outlined in this section, or, better yet, help them come up with their own ideas for activities.

Art Activities

MATERIALS

- ✓ *recycled paper bags*
- ✓ *paste*
- ✓ *scrap materials such as feathers, tissue paper, pieces of ribbon, string, yarn, etc.*
- ✓ *shoe boxes*
- ✓ *natural and recycled materials, such as clay, grass, twigs, cutouts, recycled materials, etc.*

- Ask students to design animal masks using recycled paper bags, feathers, tissue paper, pieces of ribbon, string, yarn, etc. Display the masks on the classroom walls.
- Show students how to build dioramas using old shoe boxes, clay, grass, twigs, cutouts, recycled materials, etc. This can be an individual, paired, or group project.
- Work with groups to make your own pop-up books of animals. Give each group a pop-up book to use as a model. Each group can choose one animal and figure out how to use heavy construction paper to make it stand up on the page. Display the finished products in the library or in another public place in the school.

MATERIALS

- ✓ *coat hangers*
- ✓ *string*
- ✓ *animal pictures*
- ✓ *laminating materials*

- Have the class construct mobiles. For example, a food chain mobile might have pictures of a polar bear, a seal, and a fish. Use colored paper to form the animals or cut them out of magazines and newspapers. Laminate each piece, attach it to a coat hanger with a string, and suspend the coat hanger from the ceiling.

MATERIALS
- ✓ pieces of cloth or paper
- ✓ styrofoam peanuts
- ✓ glue

- Make stuffed animals in class. Use styrofoam packing material broken into small pieces for the stuffing. Have students draw and then cut out two identical animal shapes from cloth or paper. Then have them glue the edges together, leaving a small opening. Drop pieces of styrofoam through the opening, press the edges together, and seal the opening with glue. Group similar types of animals together and display them in the classroom.
- Show students how to create word pictures by writing the name of an animal on a piece of paper and then embellishing each letter of the word. (See the example below.) Later you can laminate these word pictures and make a booklet out of them. Display the booklet in the reading corner so all students can have a chance to spend some time looking at it.

MATERIALS
- ✓ plastic cans, jugs, bottles, boxes, or other recycled containers
- ✓ glue
- ✓ crayons
- ✓ recycled scrap materials

- Make animal sculptures out of discarded materials. Ask students to bring to class plastic cans, jugs, bottles, boxes, etc. that have been emptied and cleaned. Have them design an animal of their choice using these containers and then add details using scraps of paper, crayons, aluminum foil, and recycled materials. Display this Recycled Menagerie in a Recycling Corner.

Wildlife Awareness

Using Videos. There are a number of excellent videos and television series that emphasize the importance of saving endangered species from extinction. (According to some sources, it appears that, by the close of this century, 100 animal species a day may be facing this fate.) Show one of these videos in class or ask students to watch a similar television program with their families. Then have students work in groups to write short letters to area legislators or newspapers about what they think people in the community could do to help protect these animals.

Launch a Clean-Up Campaign

- Discuss the relationship between a clean environment and a healthy wildlife population. Point out that litter, especially plastic and metal waste, is dangerous to birds and small animals. Leftover cleaning products which are improperly disposed of pollute waterways, causing fish and birds to become sick and die.
- Help students plan a Clean-up Campaign for the area around the school or elsewhere in the community. Beginning level students can make posters announcing the time and place. More advanced students can write letters inviting other teachers and members of the community to participate. Students can also visit local businesses in person, asking for support in the form of donations of bags and brooms to use during the clean-up.

Promote Recycling. Point out that the recycling of newspapers and other paper products slows down the deforestation process and preserves wildlife habitats. Ask students to find out what the recycling rules are in your community. What kinds of materials are accepted? When are they picked up? Where can they be dropped off? Then have students work in groups to create informational flyers. Duplicate them and suggest that students put them on bulletin boards and pass them out to friends and family members.

Animal Booklets

MATERIALS

✓ *Animal Booklet reproducible masters, pages 97–102*

After having developed some new language, students will enjoy making their own booklets about animals. Make copies of the "Animal Booklet" on pages 97–102 and distribute the pages to all students. I have found that animal booklets work especially well with intermediate and advanced second and third graders.

Have each student choose a favorite animal to write about. Then help them find appropriate sources of information so that they can experience success as they research the facts they need to complete their booklets. Encourage group work so that students can share ideas on where and how to find data for these books. When the booklets are complete, read some of them to the class and display them in the reading corner so that everyone has a chance to look at them.

Animal Riddles

Pair Work. Tell students to choose an animal and think of three words or phrases to describe it—how it looks, how it sounds, where it lives, what it eats, etc. Then have them write three clues to the identity of the animal in the first person, saving the best clue for last. (For example: *I am brown and white. I have four legs. I give milk. What am I?*) After they have written their three clues on a piece of paper, have them take another sheet of paper of the same size and draw a picture of the animal in its natural habitat. Attach the clue sheet on top of the picture so that the person trying to solve the riddle can lift the paper and find the answer.

I am yellow.
I have a big mane.
I live in Africa.
What am I?

page 1

page 2

An Animal Riddle
Lien Le , Age 7

MATERIALS
- ✓ *paper*
- ✓ *pencils*
- ✓ *wallpaper*
- ✓ *stapler*

A Riddle Booklet. Have students work with partners and write animal riddles, describing each animal using a maximum of five sentences. Then ask them to write the answer on the back of the paper. Collect the riddles and publish them in booklet form. Make a wallpaper cover for the booklets and display them in the library.

MATERIALS
- ✓ drawing paper
- ✓ posterboard
- ✓ scissors
- ✓ glue
- ✓ laminating materials
- ✓ self-sealing plastic bags

Animal Jigsaw Puzzles

Ask students to draw and color a habitat they have researched, such as the Arctic tundra, the Asian jungle, the Brazilian rain forest, etc., including some animals that live there. Use 8½-by-ll-inch sheets of paper. Glue each one on light posterboard. Then laminate them and cut them into several pieces to create animal puzzles. Store each one in a self-sealing plastic bag.

Charts, Cards, and Drawings

Top Ten Animal Chart. Make a list of the students' ten favorite animals. Then ask them to make a bar graph comparing the sizes of all the animals. Post the graph on the bulletin board and encourage students to look it over.

Two-Faced Animal Cards. Brainstorm a list of animal names that have more than one meaning (for example: *bat, bear,* and *crane).* Give each student a piece of construction paper folded in two. Ask each student to choose one animal from the list that has been compiled and to illustrate the two meanings of the word. Have them add sentences using the target word under both pictures. Display the cards in the classroom.

The bat flies in The sky.

I play baseball with a bat.

A Two-Faced Animal Card
Cecilia Ortiz, Age 8

Full-Size Animal Art. Give students a chance to use their artistic, scientific, and mathematical skills to produce life-size drawings of animals on butcher paper or other large art paper. First

MATERIALS
- ✓ rulers
- ✓ butcher paper
- ✓ markers
- ✓ laminating materials
- ✓ reference books about animals and their habitats

they can use reference books to look up the measurements of their animals. Then they can use mathematics to determine the proportions of their animals. They may have to solve problems such as: *How long should I make the elk's antlers?* (If the elk in the picture measures 3 inches high with 1½-inch antlers, students will learn that their enlarged version must have antlers that are half as wide as the animal is tall.) Then students are ready to draw or paint their life-size animals. Have them cut out the animals and laminate them, if possible. Once the animal drawings are complete, students can draw upon their research and recreate the animals' habitat.

GETTING FAMILIES INVOLVED

Whenever possible, give homework assignments that will involve family members in the educational process. People who live with the student are very important in helping them develop vocabulary and thinking skills, and can do a lot to instill a sense of pride in the student's cultural heritage. Some ideas are described here, but the list is almost endless.

Charting Animal Sounds

Ask students to interview family members and learn the sounds animals make in their native language. Encourage students to record the sounds on a tape recorder. They can then transcribe them into English and fill out a chart like the one on the next page. Compare the lists brought in by students from various countries and look for similarities and differences.

Singing and Dancing

Have students ask family members to teach them a song or a dance about an animal that is familiar in their native country. Then ask them to sing it for the rest of the class and explain what it is about. If they do not wish to sing in front of the class, they might make recordings of their families or themselves singing it. An example is the pajarito dance of Mexico.

Animals	English	French	Spanish	Lao
cat	meow	miaou	miau	meow (meaou)
cow	moo	meu	mū	mōō mōō
dog	bow-wow	wouf, wouf	ua-ua	gnong
donkey	he-haw	hi-han	io (ēo)	—
duck	quack	coin-coin	kwa-kwa	kwēck
rooster	cock-a-doodle-doo	cocorico	ki kiri ki	aok ē ōwn oak
sheep	baa-baa	bê... bê...	bâ bâ	bê bê

A Chart of Animal Sounds

Looking at Proverbs about Animals

Ask students to collaborate with family members and make a list of native language colloquial expressions and proverbs involving animals. They can be written down in the native language and students can then translate them into English with the help of a partner. Expressions like these provide a window onto contrasting world cultures. Post the list on a bulletin board. Ask students to illustrate some of the expressions on posterboard for a wild-looking bulletin board.

CONCLUSION

All animals are essential in the environmental balance. As mankind settles and develops the planet, many species are becoming endangered. By developing our students' interest in animals, we can help them understand the importance of saving wetlands and other wildlife habitats that shelter these endangered species.

The study of animals can also help students expand their language, strengthen their math skills, and quench their thirst for scientific knowledge. In addition, through reading and research, individually and in groups, students improve their research skills and are exposed to some excellent examples of literature from around the world.

SUGGESTED READINGS

(Titles mentioned in this chapter are marked with a ♦.)

Aardema, Verna. *Borreguita and the Coyote.* New York: Alfred A. Knopf, 1991. (Mexico; A Junior Literary Guild Selection)

———. *Traveling to Tondo, A Tale of the Nkundo of Zaire.* New York: Alfred A. Knopf, 1991.

Adams, Robin. *The Rabbit Visits the Dragon King.* Seoul, Korea: Yangjisa & Co., Inc., 1968. (Korea)

Addison-Wesley, *The Addison-Wesley Picture Dictionary.* Reading, MA, 1984.

Alexander, Ellen. *Llama and the Great Flood.* New York: Thomas Y. Crowell, 1989.

Appleby, Ellen. *The Three Billy-Goats Gruff.* New York: Scholastic, 1984.

Argueta, Manlio. *Magic Dogs of the Volcanoes.* San Francisco: Children's Book Press, 1990.

♦ ASPCA. *The Animal Rights Handbook, Everyday Ways To Save Animal Lives.* Los Angeles: Living Planet Press, 1990.

Averoux, Pierre, and Molinard, Isabelle. *Animals of the Tropics.* Englewood Cliffs, New Jersey: Silver Burdett Press, 1989.

Bancroft, Henrietta and Van Gelder, Richard. *Animals in the Winter.* New York: Thomas Y. Crowell, 1963.

Bonners, Susan. *A Penguin Year.* New York: A Dell Young Yearling Special, 1981. (Winner of the American Book Award)

Blood, Charles L. and Link, Martin. *The Goat in the Rug.* New York: Alladin Books, 1990.

♦ Brett, Jan. *The Mitten, a Ukrainian Folktale.* New York: G. P. Putnam's Sons, 1989. (The Ukraine)

Brown, Marcia. *Once a Mouse.* New York: Aladdin Books, 1961. (Winner of the Caldecott Medal)

Bruchac, Joseph. *Native American Stories.* Golden, Colorado: Fulcrum Publishing Co., 1991. (Native American)

Cohen, Caron Lee. *The Mud Pony*. New York: Scholastic, 1988. (Native American)

Cohlene, Terri. *Ka-ha-si and the Loon,* an Eskimo Legend. Mahwah, New Jersey: Watermill Press, 1990. (Eskimo)

Cole, Joanna. *Hungry, Hungry Sharks.* New York: Random House, 1986.

Davis, Grania. *The King and the Mangoes.* Emeryville, California: Dharma Publishing, 1975. (Laos)

Day, Jennifer W. *What Is a Mammal?* Racine, Wisconsin: Western Publishing Co., 1975.

Demi. *Demi's Reflective Tales.* New York: Grosset & Dunlap, 1988. (China)

Evans, Mariam. *When the Elephants Came.* Washington, D. C.: Mage Publishers, 1988. (Iran)

Dorros, Arthur. *Rain Forest Secrets.* New York: Scholastic, 1990.

◆ Galdone, Paul. *Three Aesop Fox Fables.* New York: Seabury Press, 1971.

Goble, Paul. *Dream Wolf.* New York: Bradbury Press, 1990.

———. *The Girl Who Loved Wild Horses.* New York: Alladin Books, 1978. (Winner of the Caldecott Medal and an ALA Notable Book Award)

Grant, Joan. *The Monster That Grew Small.* New York: Lothrop, Lee & Shepard Books, 1987. (Egypt)

Greaves, Nick. *When Hippo Was Hairy and Other Tales from Africa.* New York: Barron's Educational Series, 1988. (Africa)

◆ Hogrogian, Nonny. *One Fine Day.* New York: Collier Books, 1971. (Winner of the Caldecott Medal)

◆ Huynh, Quang Nhuong. *The Land I Lost.* New York: Harper Trophy, 1982. (Vietnam)

Isenbart, Hans-Heinrich. *A Duckling Is Born.* New York: G. P. Putnam's Sons, 1979.

Jataka Tales. *The Rabbit in the Moon*. Oakland, California: Dharma Press, 1989.

◆ Johnston, Tony. *Badger and the Magic Fan.* New York: G. P. Putnam's Sons, 1990.

King, Deborah. *Cloudy.* New York: Philomel Books, 1990.

King, Kay. *Shanta, Sunil and the Cobra.* New York: Abelard-Schuman, 1968.

Kipling, Rudyard. *The Elephant's Child.* New York: Harcourt Brace Jovanovich, 1983.

Krumgold, Joseph. *...and now Miguel.* New York: Harper Trophy, 1953.

◆ Leaf, Munro. *The Story of Ferdinand.* New York: Puffin Books, 1936.

Lifton, Betty Jean. *Kap and the Wicked Monkey*. New York: Grosset & Dunlap, 1968.

———. *The Many Lives of Chio and Goro.* New York: W. W. Norton, 1968.

Mark, David. *The Sheep of the Lal Bagh.* New York: Parents' Magazine Press, 1967.

◆ Matthews, Peter (ed.). *The Guinness Book of Records.* New York: Bantam Books, 1993.

◆ Mitchell, Lucy Sprague. *Another Here and Now Storybook.* New York: E.P. Dutton, 1937, 1965.

Momaday, Natachee Scott. *Owl in the Cedar Tree.* Lincoln, Nebraska: University of Nebraska Press, 1975.

Namjoshi, Suniti. *Aditi and the One-Eyed Monkey.* Boston: Beacon Press, 1986.

Parnwell, E.C. *The New Oxford Picture Dictionary.* New York: Oxford University Press, 1988.

Paterson, Katherine. *The Tale of the Mandarin Ducks.* New York: Scholastic, 1990.

◆ Pollock, Yvonne. *The Old Man's Mitten.* New York: Scholastic, 1986.

Posell, Elsa. *Cats.* Chicago: Children's Press, 1983.

Prelutsky, Jack. *Read-Aloud Rhymes for the Very Young.* New York: Alfred A. Knopf, 1986.

Schnieper, Claudia. *On the Trail of the Fox.* Minneapolis, Minnesota: Caroleshade Books, Inc., 1986.

Selsam, Millicent. *A First Look at Snakes, Lizards, and other Reptiles.* New York: Walker Publishing, 1975.

Shannon, Terry. *A Dog Team for Ongluk.* Chicago: Melmont Publishers, 1962. (Eskimo)

———. *A Playmate for Puna.* Chicago: Melmont Publishers, 1963.

Standiford, Natalie. *The Bravest Dog Ever.* New York: Random House, 1989.

Terada, Alice M. *Under the Starfruit Tree.* Honolulu: University of Hawaii Press, 1989. (Vietnam)

- Wall, Lina Mao. *Judge Rabbit and the Tree Spirit.* San Francisco: Children's Book Press, 1991. (Cambodia)

Wells, Rosemary. *Abdul.* New York: Dial Books for Young Readers, 1970.

- Xiong, Blia. *Nine-In-One, Grr! Grr!* San Francisco: Children's Book Press, 1989. (Laos)

ADDITIONAL RESOURCES AND SERIES

Smallwood, Betty Ansin. *The Literature Connection: A Read-Aloud Guide for Multicultural Classrooms.* Reading, MA: Addison-Wesley, 1991. (This annotated guide to multicultural literature lists additional titles in its sections on Animals, pages 157–172, and Imagination/Monsters/Magic, pages 186–190.)

Animals in the Wild. New York: Scholastic. (A series of books for young children which shows each animal in its natural surroundings and describes its life and its struggle for survival.)

The *Little Bear* series. New York: Harper Trophy.

The *Frog and Toad* series. New York: Harper Trophy.

The *Curious George* series. Boston: Houghton Mifflin.

The *Nature's Children* series. Danbury, Connecticut: Grolier.

The National Wildlife Federation, 8925 Leesburg Pike, Vienna, Virginia, 22184

Nature Conservancy, 1815 N. Lynn Street, Arlington, Virginia, 22209

ANIMALS FROM MY COUNTRY

Name_______________________ Date ____________

THINGS ANIMALS CAN DO

Name________________________________ Date ______________

Can Live on Land	
Can Run	
Can Swim	
Can Fly	
Can Hop	

THINGS ANIMALS HAVE

Name ______________________ Date ____________

Have Sharp Claws	
Have Long Tails	
Have Spots	
Have Stripes	

COMPARATIVES AND SUPERLATIVES

Name_______________________________ Date ______________

Fill in the blanks with the correct form of the adjective.

fast 1. The Peregrine falcon reaches 200 miles an hour or more as it dives or swoops down on prey. It is probably the ______________ of all American birds.

big 2. The black bear is the ______________ of all the bears.

swift 3. The cheetah is one of the ______________ mammals.

tall 4. The camel is ______________ than the goat, but not ______________ tall ______________ the giraffe.

poisonous 5. The puffer fish is one of the ______________________ fish.

expensive 6. In Japan, it is ______________________ to eat puffer fish or "fugu" fish.

strong 7. The tiger is the ______________ cat of all.

fluffy 8. The feathers of the ostrich are ______________ than those of the Andean condor.

bad 9. The lives of animals in a circus are ______________ than those of animals in a zoo.

Animals

by ______________________________

The Animal I Am Writing About

The name of my animal is

______________________________.

This animal lives on the continent of

______________________________.

Draw an illustration of your animal.

All About My Animal

This is what my animal looks like as a baby.

This is what my animal looks like when it is full grown.

Food for My Animal

What is the main food of your animal? Write the words here.

Draw some pictures of foods your animal likes to eat. Write the name of the food under its picture.

About My Animal's Home

Draw a picture of your animal's home.

Describe your animal's home.

Is there anything special about your animal's home?

Special Facts About My Animal

As you researched your animal, you may have discovered interesting and unique facts about your animal. You may have found some information that you did not know about your animal that you can share with your friends. Remember you are the "expert" on this animal. Write down some unique and interesting facts about your animal.

INTERNATIONAL FOODS
Chapter
4
FROM FRIJOLES TO DAL

CONTENT AREA LEARNING WEB

INTERNATIONAL FOODS

SCIENCE

Planting crops in class, 106
Making Stone Soup, 106
Comparing tastes, 107
Tasting wheat bread, 107
Making butter, 107
Discussing four basic tastes, 109
Making a Sweet-Sour Taste Chart, 109
Investigating sugar, 118–119
Investigating chocolate, 120
Investigating peanuts, 120
Discussing the food pyramid, 121–122

MATH

Creating a Sorting Foods Chart, 108
Mass and count nouns, 110
Estimating, 111
Comparing metric and U.S. weights and measures, 111–112
Making a bar graph, 121
Using coupons to understand price comparisons, 121
Making pie graphs, 122–123

LANGUAGE ARTS

Reading aloud, 106
Sorting and classifying foods, 108
Labeling pictures of food, 108
Describing meals, 108–109
Developing food-related vocabulary, 108–110
Prefixes and suffixes, 110
Identifying opposites, 109
Mass and count nouns, 110
Plurals with -es, 110
Pronouncing the letters oo, 110–111
Food word search, 116
Making a class cookbook, 124–125

SOCIAL STUDIES

Field trip to the grocery store, 107
Discussing the school menu, 107
Listing foods from around the world, 109
Comparing ways of setting a table, 109
Making a Bread Web, 112
Brainstorming: Bread around the world, 112
Making a Corn Web, 113
Comparing foo-foo recipes, 117
Poll of class favorites, 121
Doing research projects, 122–123
Making a class cookbook, 124–125

ART AND MUSIC

Favorite foods display, 106
Wall hanging display, 106
International cookbooks display, 106
Meals of the Day Chart, 106
Drawing international foods, 109
Drawing story characters, 114

READING COMPREHENSION

Listening to stories, 106
Listening for repetition, rhythm, and rhyme, 106
Introducing the concept of story characters, 114
Reading non-fiction books about food, 114–115, 119–120
Reading stories about food, 113–118
Sequencing/Making lists, 116–117
Developing a Table of Facts, 117–118
Reading for information, 118
Discussing similarities and differences, 118–119
Doing research projects, 122–123

FAMILY INVOLVEMENT

Planning potluck meals, 124
Making a class cookbook, 124–125
Cooking utensils from around the world, 125

CHAPTER 4. INTERNATIONAL FOODS

Âman, iman ah, isûdâr.

Water is life; milk is food.

—TUAREG PROVERB

While you may have to expend considerable energy to generate interest in some topics, this is never the case with food. Food, like shelter, is a basic necessity that all students are aware of—some of them painfully so. I have taught Cambodian students who survived on roots as they were fleeing from their war-torn country over a decade ago and who, unfortunately, still suffer from the effects of malnutrition. Many of our students—those with limited English proficiency and others—arrive in classrooms having experienced the pangs of hunger. Sadly, the number of those children depending upon the school lunch as their one solid meal of the day keeps on increasing.

The title of this unit reminds us that students who come from other cultures and other countries have widely differing tastes in food. When they eat lunch in the school cafeteria, most gladly choose a hamburger, a hot dog, or a slice of pizza. But if you were to see what they ask for at home, it is much more likely that it would be *arroz y frijoles, papas á la Jun Kina,* or *dal bhat.*

This unit on food will take us on a culinary tour around the world. It will provide an opportunity for students to compare the foods of their native countries with those of other countries. They will learn what constitutes a healthy diet and will experiment with various systems of weights and measures. They will do some research on major food crops and reflect on the world's dwindling food resources. The unit ends with a potluck supper. Here students and their families can share their favorite foods with others in the class and celebrate the diversity of flavors they bring to the dinner table.

SPARKING INTEREST

Students usually don't need much encouragement to start thinking and talking about food. The kinds of displays and activities you introduce in this section should be specially designed to get them interested in the variety of foods people in other parts of the world eat, and to start them thinking about where our food comes from and why some people don't get enough to eat.

Using Visual Stimuli

- Turn a corner of the bulletin board into an Art Corner where students can pin up pictures of favorite foods they have cut out of magazines. If you wish, you can designate several areas for different types of foods—fruits, vegetables, grains, desserts, complete meals, etc.
- If you can find one, display an *arpillera* (an embroidered wall hanging from South America) or a *paj ntaub* (made by the Hmong of Laos) with a country scene showing people working in the fields and going to market.
- In the Book Corner, set up a display of international cookbooks from the library and from students' homes. Encourage students to browse through the books, looking at pictures of familiar and unfamiliar foods.

READING

- ✓ The Little Red Hen *(any version)*
- ✓ Everybody Cooks Rice, *by Norah Dooley*
- ✓ Strega Nona, *by Tomie de Paola*
- ✓ Cloudy With a Chance of Meatballs, *by Judy Barrett*

Using Auditory Stimuli

Read aloud some of the following books: *The Little Red Hen* (any version); *Everybody Cooks Rice,* by Norah Dooley; *Strega Nona,* by Tomie de Paola; or *Cloudy With a Chance of Meatballs,* by Judy Barrett. Have students listen for repeated words, phrases, or rhythms.

MATERIALS

- ✓ *beans or corn seed*
- ✓ *pots for planting*
- ✓ *potting soil*
- ✓ *potato, sweet potato, or avocado pit*
- ✓ *water glass or glass jar*

MATERIALS

- ✓ *vegetables to make soup*
- ✓ *an electric slow cooker*
- ✓ *a smooth, clean stone*
- ✓ Stone Soup *(any version)*

Using Kinesthetic Stimuli

- Let students observe the beginnings of new plant life. Bring in beans or corn seed, pots, and soil. Have students plant a food crop and watch it begin to grow. Or have students place potatoes, sweet potatoes, or avocado pits in a partially-filled water glass and watch roots develop.
- After reading the old French tale, *Stone Soup,* make a list of the vegetables needed and ask each student to each bring one of them to class. The next day, cut up the vegetables, put them in an electric slow cooker, add a smooth, clean stone, and simmer the soup until it is ready to eat.

- Take children on a trip to a local grocery store or a farm market. Carry a basket or string bag and have children pick out foods that they can taste when you are back in school.

Using Gustatory Stimuli

MATERIALS
- ✓ *red apples and green apples*
- ✓ *raw and cooked samples of a single vegetable*
- ✓ *apricots and dried apricots*
- ✓ *other pairs of foods*

- Bring to class red apples and green apples, raw and cooked vegetables, apricots and dried apricots, and other pairs of foods. Try to include a variety of textures (crisp, crunchy, soft, wet, or dry) and a variety of tastes (sweet, sour, bitter, spicy, or bland). Have students taste and compare the various pairs, discussing the differences in texture and flavor.

MATERIALS
- ✓ *ingredients and equipment needed for making bread*
- ✓ The Little Red Hen *(any version)*
- ✓ *whipping cream*
- ✓ *a glass jar with a tight-fitting cover*
- ✓ The Dragon Kite, *by Thomas Lewis*

- Bake whole wheat bread and distribute it to students after you finish reading *The Little Red Hen.* If you don't have the facilities for making bread, visit a bakery and bring bread into your classroom that is fresh from the oven. Children will enjoy the warmth and the aroma of the fresh-baked loaves.
- Have students take turns shaking a jar of cream until it turns to butter. Have students taste the finished product after you finish reading *The Dragon Kite,* by Thomas Lewis.

EXPANDING LANGUAGE

Newcomers receive an introduction to food on the very first day of school. New students often look bewildered as they are asked if they want to "buy lunch" or if they are on "free lunch." In order to address their immediate food-related needs, assign each new student a "buddy" who may, or may not, speak the newcomer's language, but who will provide assistance to his or her partner. As they go through the lunch line together, both will benefit from the experience of asking and answering questions about food.

It is a good idea to post the weekly or monthly menu on the bulletin board so that students can get an idea of what kinds of foods will be served. Take a few moments each day to write out the day's menu on the board and discuss such puzzling terms as *chicken fingers* and *s'mores.* Whenever possible, display pictures to accompany the words and encourage students to comment about their special likes and dislikes.

Developing Vocabulary

MATERIALS

- ✓ a basket of fruits and vegetables, including imported items
- ✓ cans and packages of food
- ✓ containers that food comes in
- ✓ transparent plastic canisters containing dried foods of various colors
- ✓ pictures of various food items

Introduce the names of a variety of basic foods, using real fruits and vegetables and prepared food items. Magazine illustrations and picture cards will help fill in when it isn't practical to bring the actual item to the classroom. The National Dairy Council can also supply large, colorful pictures with magnets on the backs. These are useful for creating blackboard displays and for use in cooperative learning projects. Ask the students who have mastered the assigned vocabulary in record time to become "teacher's assistants" and provide individual help to other students.

- Once everyone knows the basic vocabulary, invite students to work in pairs to sort the foods into categories such as fruits, vegetables, meats, grains, etc. Later, conduct an oral review of the names of all the foods and switch to written exercises.

MATERIALS

- ✓ "Sorting Foods" reproducible master, page 130
- ✓ a picture dictionary

- Make copies of "Sorting Foods" on page 130 and distribute them to all students. Ask them to look up as many foods as they can in a picture dictionary and list them in the appropriate columns on the handout. (Students who experience difficulty writing, but who like to draw, should be encouraged to do just that; they will still learn something in the process.)
- Use the Sorting Foods chart for further discussion and classification. Ask: *Which fruits are red? Which fruits are green? Which vegetables grow in your country? Which vegetables grow on the ground? Which ones grow under the ground?, etc.*

MATERIALS

- ✓ construction paper
- ✓ crayons or markers
- ✓ pictures of various food items
- ✓ paste

- Give each student a piece of construction paper (or recycled paper) and ask them to divide it into three parts representing the three meals of the day. Have them label the sections *breakfast, lunch,* and *dinner.* Suggest that they draw a clock at the top of each section to show what time of day each meal is eaten. Then ask them to cut out food pictures from magazines and paste them in the appropriate section. Draw a sample illustration on the board to show students what their completed charts might look like. Suggest that they write a sentence or two about each picture. For example: *I eat breakfast at 7:00 a.m. I drink orange juice. I eat a tortilla.* This is a good time to discuss the importance of a good breakfast and to be on the lookout for students who might be candidates for a free breakfast program.

- Distribute sheets of paper on which you have drawn squares. Ask students to draw pictures of fruits and vegetables from their native countries or local areas. Encourage them to write the name of each item in their native language (or in English, if they can). You might start by brainstorming and listing on the board some examples of foods from a particular country.

MATERIALS
- ✓ *plates, cups, and glasses*
- ✓ *knives, forks, and spoons*
- ✓ *chopsticks*

- Talk about place settings. This activity enables students to expand their vocabulary, practice prepositions of place, and compare and contrast customs around the world. Use actual plates, cups, cutlery, chopsticks, etc. Ask each person to set a place as they would in their own homes. Ask questions that will elicit the use of the present progressive tense and prepositions of place. For example: *I am placing the knife to the right of the plate. I am putting the napkin next to the plate.* If you ask the right questions, you may find that some students do not use any cutlery, and instead use chopsticks, chappatis, or tortillas to pick up food.

MATERIALS
- ✓ *"Sweet/Sour Chart" reproducible master, page 131*
- ✓ *sweet, sour, salty, and bitter foods*

- Discuss the four basic tastes: *sweet, sour, salty,* and *bitter.* Make copies of the "Sweet/Sour Chart" on page 131 and distribute them to all students. Then have a food-tasting party in the Science Corner and record the results of your research on the chart. Later, write in more foods on the chart and expand the list of descriptors to include some of the following: *raw/cooked, salty/bland, ripe/unripe, fresh/stale, tasty/tasteless, fat/lean, well-done/rare, light/heavy, tender/tough,* and *crisp/soggy.*

MATERIALS
- ✓ *"Opposites" reproducible master, page 132*

- Make copies of "Opposites" on page 132 and distribute them to all students. Ask them to complete the chart individually and then bring it to you so that you can review their work with them.

- You can develop abstract vocabulary with intermediate and advanced students by focusing on certain prefixes or suffixes. In this unit, you might start with the prefix *pre-,* as in *pre-cook, preheat,* and *preset.* The suffix *-ous,* as in *nutritious, delicious,* and *scrumptious* could also be used to further develop vocabulary connected with the topic of food.

Developing Language

Mass Nouns and Count Nouns

MATERIALS

✓ *pictures or actual samples of countable foods (oranges, eggs, etc.) and uncountable foods (rice, milk, etc.)*

- The topic of food lends itself well to work on mass nouns and count nouns. Use realia or visual aids to teach (or review) the use of the singular or plural with fruits, vegetables, and other foods. Use sentences such as: *How many oranges are there in a dozen? How much water is there in the glass? How many eggs are there in a carton? and How much soup is there in this can?* Demonstrate that it is easy to count apples and yams, but almost impossible to count water or rice. Ask pairs to work together to make lists of all the food-related mass nouns and count nouns they can think of.

MATERIALS

✓ *"Hamud's Bag and Basket" reproducible master, page 133*

- Make copies of "Hamud's Bag and Basket" on page 133 and distribute them to all students. Ask them to write the names of the count nouns on the basket and the mass nouns on the bag. Go over the completed handouts together in class.

MATERIALS

✓ *"Rukhamini's Favorite Fruit" reproducible master, page 134*

***Plurals with* -es.** This is also a good time to introduce the *-es* plural. Point out that you usually add *-es* to words ending in *sh, ch, ss,* and *o* to make the plural. Elicit examples such as *radishes, matches, glasses,* and *potatoes* and make a list on the board. Make copies of "Rukhamini's Favorite Fruit" on page 134 and distribute them to all students. Ask them to work in pairs to complete the handout. Go over the completed handouts with the class.

***Pronunciation of* oo.** Start off an activity on the two pronunciations of *oo* using the words *cook* and *food.* Write the two words on the blackboard and ask students to brainstorm as many other words as possible formed with the double *o.* Encourage them to skim through their writing and current reading or basal textbooks as you make up the list. Discuss the words and ask students to help you group them under two columns corresponding to the long and short vowel sounds. Some long *oo* words: *food, mood, soon, spoon, balloon,* and *zoo.* Some short *oo* words: *cook, hook, book, look, nook, took, shook, crook* and *brook*.

Math Activities

The following activities give every student a chance to practice mathematics, develop estimation skills, and recognize that all cultures and customs are accepted and valued in a global classroom.

MATERIALS
✓ *a variety of different types of beans*
✓ *several different glass jars*

Estimating. If available, use *masoor dal* (red lentils) and various colors and sizes of dried beans such as *frijoles negros* for this activity. First count the beans carefully and write down the numbers. Put different quantities of beans in variously-shaped glass jars. Invite students to estimate the number of beans in each jar and write their guesses on squares of recycled paper. Announce the winners at the end of the week. To make the activity even more interesting, you can invite students to bring in their own jars filled with beans from their native countries and have you, the teacher, join in the estimation contest.

Using the Metric System

MATERIALS
✓ *a balance scale*
✓ *metric weights*
✓ *food items to weigh*
✓ *pound and ounce weights*

- Obtain a balance and a set of gram and kilogram weights. Display such grocery items as bags of polenta, brown rice, stone-ground flour, macaroni, etc. in various boxes and bags. First ask students to estimate the weight of the grocery items. Then ask them to weigh each one on the scales to check their predictions. Have them make a list of each item, their estimation of its weight, and its actual weight.
- Bring in a set of ounce and pound weights and ask students to use a balance scale to compare metric and U.S. weights. First have them see how much a pound and ounce are in metric terms. Then suggest that they see how much a gram and a kilogram are in U.S. terms. They can then make a chart summarizing the equivalencies they have discovered.

MATERIALS
✓ *a metric ruler and a meter stick*
✓ *a ruler and a yardstick showing inches and feet*

- Have students measure several items (such as the height of the door, the size of their desk tops, the length of a pencil, etc.) first in centimeters and meters, and then in inches and feet. Suggest that they make a three-column chart listing each item, its metric measurements, and its dimensions in inches and feet.

Bread: A Global Perspective

- Write three words for *bread* on the board (*bread* is English, *Brot* is German, and *brood* is Dutch). Ask students what they call *bread* in their language. They will discover that different languages use different versions of the same basic word. Then help them make a Bread Web. Start with the Latin word *panus* and draw a Bread Web showing the word for *bread* in several different languages. (You can choose a few items from the drawing below to get started.) Invite students to add spokes to the chart with their own individual contributions.

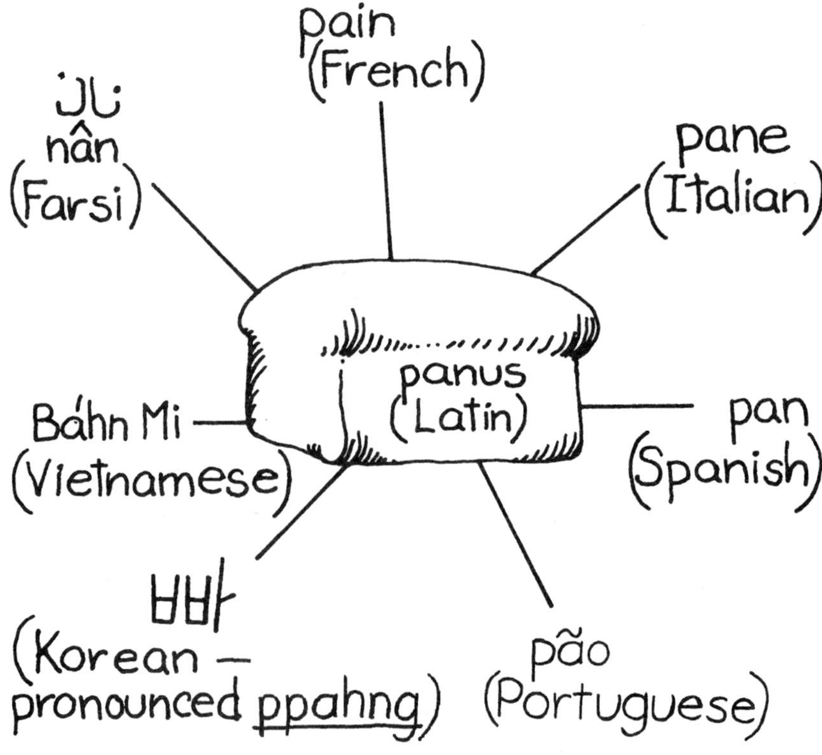

A Bread Web

- Brainstorm with the class a list of specific types of bread eaten around the world. Discuss the ingredients that go into each one and how each one tastes. The list may include: *challah, lavash, pita, chappati, nan, puri, pizza, tortilla, ficelle, baguette,* and *lahmajun.*

The Many Uses of Corn

Encourage students to think about how many different foods can be produced from a single source by creating a Corn Web with them. Draw an ear of corn on the board and ask them to come to the board and list all the foods they know of that come from corn. Use the sample below as a beginning.

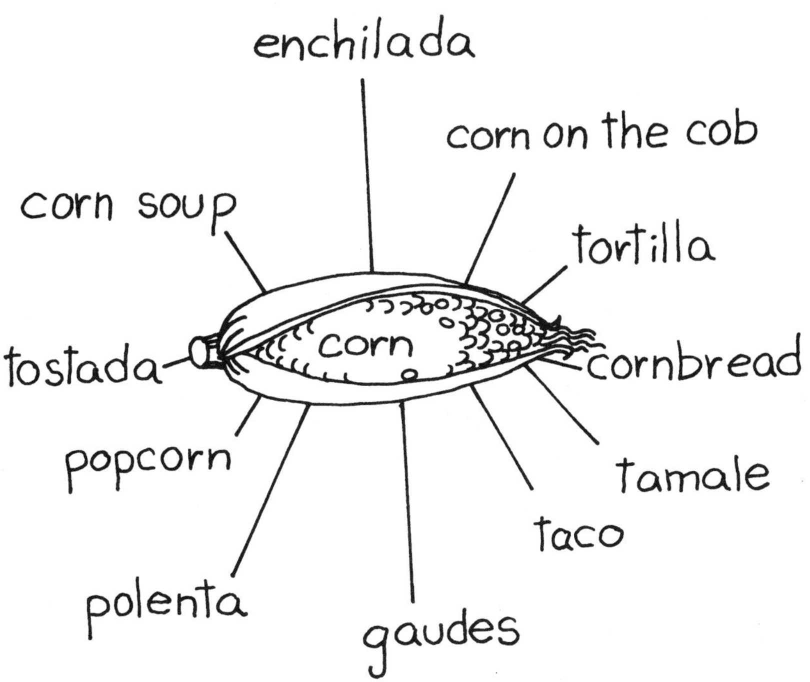

A Web of Foods Made From Corn

READING AND REFLECTING

Food is a recurring topic in our daily lives and in literature. On winter nights, I never drink my *tisane de tilleul* (herb tea) without thinking of one of my favorite writers, Marcel Proust, who suddenly tasted the past emerge from his subconscious as he was dunking a *madeleine,* an exquisite, buttery tea cake, in his herb tea. Talk to any fan of Dr. Seuss and you will find that the strong gustatory appeal of *Green Eggs and Ham* was a definite factor in his success as an author of books for young readers.

Judging from more recent experience, my former ESL students have retained fond memories of the book *The Dragon Kite,* by Thomas Lewis, because they imitated the little Tibetan boy in the story, Kesang, and churned butter as a collaborative, culminating activity. Reading for pleasure is thus combined with reading for learning as students pull information from all sorts of stories and books—Big Books, little books, picture books, tall tales, social studies books, travel books, and fairy tales. One of my second graders was very fond of spicy food. After we read *Princess Furball,* he remarked that the reason the king married Furball was that she knew how to make good spicy soup, which tasted much better than the regular cook's soup. He had a point!

Introducing Story Elements

MATERIALS
✓ The Little Red Hen *(any version)*
✓ *story props such as a hoe, stacks of wheat, bread pan, etc.*
✓ *loaf of freshly-baked bread*

- *The Little Red Hen* always appeals to beginning students, who soon catch on to the repetitive "Not I" of the lazy animals, and the stoic "I will" of the hard-working Little Red Hen. Bring in props or pictures to illustrate the lengthy transformation of the grains of wheat into a loaf of bread. Encourage your students to draw pictures of the various steps in making bread. If possible, ask a family member to bring some freshly-baked bread to share with the class. This will undoubtedly make the Little Red Hen's reward even more telling, and it will add to the literary enjoyment of the story.

MATERIALS
✓ *drawing paper*
✓ *crayons or markers*
✓ *laminating materials*
✓ *a variety of Big Books*

- This is a good time to introduce the concept of characters. An artistic beginning student would probably welcome the opportunity to draw the various animals in the story. Laminate these pictures and place them on a bulletin board which you can then transform into a stage. As you read more Big Books, add more colorful characters to your collection from those stories. The bulletin board will enchant the students and will effortlessly teach them one of the basic elements of literature.

Using Non-Fiction

READING
✓ Let's Find Out About Bread, *by Olive Burt*
✓ Bread, *by Dorothy Turner*

- After reading *The Little Red Hen,* why not introduce simple non-fiction books, such as *Let's Find Out About Bread,* by Olive Burt, or *Bread,* by Dorothy Turner, which provides information about the history of bread? It explains about the early forms of bread in Turkey and Northern Iran, and describes different kinds of breads, leavened and unleavened, eaten

hen

dog

cat

goose

Characters from The Little Red Hen
Lien Le, Age 7

around the world. This book, written in simple language, contains clear pictures of cereal plants, such as barley, buckwheat, oats, and rye, and lends itself well to use with beginning level students.

✓ Bread Bread Bread, *by Ann Morris*

READING

- Another book, *Bread Bread Bread,* by Ann Morris, presents wonderful photographs taken by Ken Heyman of people eating or selling bread around the world. It would constitute an excellent follow-up to the etymological chart begun by students in the Expanding Language section of this chapter.

Using Fiction

- I usually try to balance the amount of fiction and non-fiction reading in my classroom. Students are always delighted with *Green Eggs and Ham,* by Dr. Seuss. *Strega Nona,* by Tomie de

READING

✓ Green Eggs and Ham, *by Dr. Seuss*

✓ Strega Nona, *by Tomie de Paola*

✓ The Magic Porridge Pot, *by Paul Galdone*

Paola, and *The Magic Porridge Pot,* a German folktale retold by Paul Galdone, make good companion books since, in both cases, incantations are needed to make the pots start boiling and stop boiling. *Strega Nona* is about a witch, Strega *(Nona* means *Grandmother),* from Calabria, Italy, whose powers enable her to make a pot boil.

- In *The Magic Porridge Pot,* not only does the pot bubble and boil, but it also supplies an abundance of food-related words. This is an opportunity too great to be missed! After reading the story together in class, draw an old-fashioned pot, add wheel-like spokes, and invite students to reread the story and list all the vocabulary related to food and cooking. Students are always enthusiastic about such a word search, and they love to write their finds on the board—especially if they are allowed to use colored chalk!

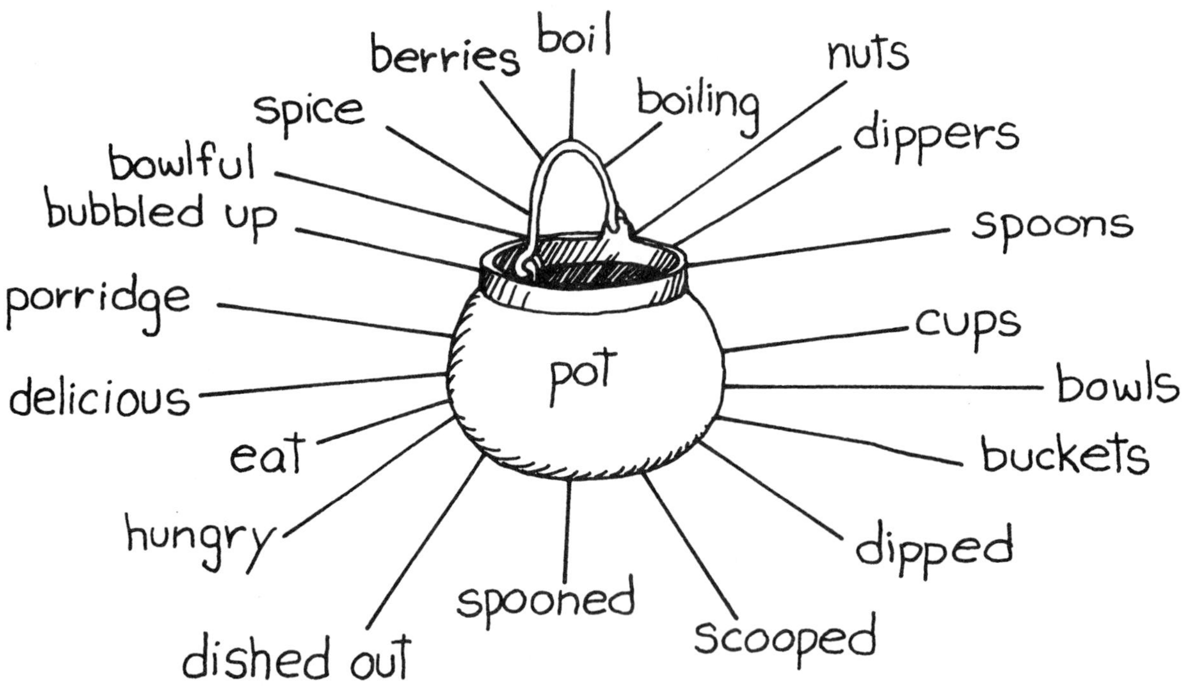

A Word Search for The Magic Porridge Pot

Using Lists

- Another way to combine pleasure and learning is to have students list important facts about the books they are reading in an organized manner. For instance, *Tonight is Carnaval,* by

✓ Tonight is Carnaval, *by Arthur Dorros*

READING

Arthur Dorros, provides an abundant supply of information about the crops grown in the Andes mountains of Peru. *Arpilleras,* sewn by women from a cooperative in Lima, Peru, illustrate the book and depict the vegetables, fruits, and lifestyle of rural Peru. Students share the impatience of the little boy who is practicing his *quena* for the joyous celebration of Carnaval. They follow the little boy's bumpy ride to town as he makes mental notes of the corn, fava beans, and other foods people are taking to market. Ask your students to make lists of the foods he notices in the order in which they appear in the story.

✓ A Drop of Honey, *by Djemma Bider*

READING

- *A Drop of Honey,* by Djemma Bider, takes us to another part of the world. There is a dream-like quality in the soft pastels used by Armen Kojoyian to illustrate this tale about Armenia. The plentiful fruits, nuts, and spices will make everyone's mouth water and every child will dream of this land of milk and honey. The author has even included the recipe for Anayida's baklava! Here students can classify the foods under headings such as *fruits, nuts,* and *spices.*

✓ The Village of Round and Square Houses, *by Ann Grifalconi*

✓ From Ashanti to Zulu, *by Margaret Musgrove*

✓ Cooking the Caribbean Way, *by Cheryl Kaufman*

READING

- *The Village of Round and Square Houses,* by Ann Grifalconi, describes life in a small village in the Cameroons, where *fou-fou* is traditionally served. Years later my students all remember *fou-fou.* In *From Ashanti to Zulu,* by Margaret Musgrove, *fou-fou* is described as being made of white yams pounded by Ga women, while a recipe for *foo foo soup*, in the cookbook *Cooking the Caribbean Way,* by Cheryl Kaufman, calls for green plantains. This cross-cultural reading and research helps students understand the importance of culinary traditions and the variations sometimes brought about by differences in climates and basic crops.

Using a Table of Facts

A Table of Facts can be used by all students from second grade on, regardless of their ability level. It provides a simple way of cataloging information from reading passages. Before reading each story, review the categories on the chart with students so that they will have in mind the kinds of facts they should be looking for as they read. This kind of charting activity helps

MATERIALS

✓ *"Table of Facts" reproducible master, page 135*

them remember information and makes it easier for them to formulate interesting comparisons and contrasts.

- Make copies of the "Table of Facts" on page 135 and distribute them to all students. Suggest that they put their names at the top and keep them in a safe place. Each time you introduce another book in class, ask them to take out their tables, review the categories, and fill in each column after finishing the story. They can then refer to the tables during class discussions or use them to write comparisons of books they have read recently.

Book Talk Activities

Students in upper grades will particularly enjoy reading in collaborative groups, and comparing notes in Book Talk sessions. In Chapter One, students focused on the weather depicted in *Little House in the Big Woods.* In this chapter on food, you might use books depicting roughly the same time period to compare crops and foods. Since students will probably need a great deal of assistance at the beginning, include vocabulary study and provide questions which will help students know where to begin their research.

READING

✓ Little House in the Big Woods, *by Laura Ingalls Wilder*

- Each time you hold a discussion, be sure to ask students to compare the lifestyle depicted in the book with their own and point out similarities and differences. Here is a sample of the kind of questions you might include for a book like *Little House in the Big Woods.*
    - For Chapter One. *List the nine vegetables that Laura and her family ate. Draw pictures of them. What kinds of meat did Laura and her family eat? How did they preserve it and store it for the winter?*
    - For Chapter Two. *Describe how Ma made butter. Did Laura and her family have electricity? How did Ma cook?*
    - For Chapter Four. *What did Ma cook for Christmas? Could Laura and the other children talk at the dinner table? Are you allowed to talk during meals?*
- Should you want to compare Laura Ingalls Wilder's portrayal of life in the woods of Wisconsin around the turn of the century with present-day life in rural Vermont, you might select

✓ Sugaring Time, *by Kathryn Lasky*

READING

the chapter "Sugar Snow," in *Little House in the Big Woods* for one group, and assign *Sugaring Time,* by Kathryn Lasky, to another group. Ask each group to read their assigned book and discuss it together.

- Below is a sample of what a simple comparison chart might look like. When students have finished their research, invite them to present their findings to the class and ask them to draw conclusions. Have methods of harvesting maple sugar changed much in the last 80 years or so? Compare the tools used, the amount of labor involved, etc.

Little House in the Big Woods (Chapter 3: Sugar Snow)	Sugaring Time
Wisconsin	Vermont
illustrations	photographs
oxen	work horses
a wooden barrel	metal pails

✓ From Beet to Sugar, *by Ali Mitgutsch*

READING

- Another group could investigate cane sugar. In addition, a group of beginning level students could easily read *From Beet to Sugar*, by Ali Mitgutsch, draw the various steps in making sugar from beets, and write simple sentences to accompany the pictures. Such a modified assignment would enable everyone to participate in the collaborative research. No doubt a student will want to reminisce about eating cane sugar in his or her native country. And as the teacher, you will probably be able to find a diplomatic way of warning your charges about the dangers of eating too much sugar.

The topic of food is as vast as the array of cookbooks now available in bookstores and it is, indeed, hard to limit oneself to a few books or stories. Your students' needs and your own tastes will ultimately determine the books you will use for this unit.

CREATING AND SHARING

You will find that many of the projects suggested in this chapter could work very well with other themes in this book. Food from plants is closely related to the plants and trees studied in Chapter Two, while food from animals could go in Chapter Three. Some books may be read at the beginning of the unit to generate interest, discussed and analyzed to expand language, and then used as springboards for further research.

Mixing Fiction and Non-Fiction

READING

✓ The Chocolate Touch, *by Patrick Catling*
✓ King Midas and the Golden Touch *(any version)*
✓ From Cacao Bean to Chocolate, *by Ali Mitgutsch*

- You can start with the ever-popular topic of chocolate! Students with good reading skills would probably enjoy *The Chocolate Touch,* by Patrick Catling. The myth of *King Midas and the Golden Touch* (with its similarities to *The Chocolate Touch)* could be assigned as follow-up reading for the most advanced group of students. Meanwhile, beginning level students might be reading *From Cacao Bean to Chocolate,* by Ali Mitgutsch. A series of drawings showing the transformation of cacao beans into chocolate would be enjoyed by all groups. Related assignments like these allow all students to be reading at a level that is challenging to them while staying on the same topic. And what could be better than a hot fudge sundae party to celebrate the completion of their projects!

READING

✓ A Pocketful of Goobers, *by Barbara Mitchell*

- Another book that provides a wealth of information on food (mainly peanuts) is the inspiring book on the life of George Washington Carver, *A Pocketful of Goobers,* by Barbara Mitchell. It appealed to my fifth-graders so much that two of them cried as they were reading about Carver's unhappy childhood. Since the period encompassed in the book is the late 1860s and the setting includes Missouri, Kansas, and Alabama, the book provides valuable social studies information and fits in well with that curriculum. A small group of intermediate level students could read the book, write about it in their Reading Logs, and discuss it in Book Talk sessions.
- For a culminating activity, ask students to design a formal menu listing all the courses served by George Washington Carver to a group of skeptical businessmen. If possible, bring

MATERIALS

✓ peanut butter cookies
✓ other non-food products made from peanuts

peanut butter cookies and other products made of peanuts to illustrate some of the 300 ways that George Washington Carver discovered the peanut could be used. (Many people are not aware that peanuts are also used to manufacture non-food products such as cosmetics.)

Activities for Beginning and Intermediate Students

Our Favorite Foods. Have the students take a class poll and come up with a list of some favorite foods and how many people like each one. Show them how to make a bar graph illustrating their findings on the board. Include ethnic foods such as rice and beans, chili con carne, Vietnamese egg rolls, Japanese plum candy, and the Indian favorite, *gulab jamun* (a kind of pastry made with rose water and honey). Use this opportunity to reflect on the fact that more and more foods are becoming "internationalized." This will foreshadow a group project, a class cookbook, in which family members will become involved.

MATERIALS

✓ food pages from a local newspaper
✓ scissors

Using Coupons. An experiential approach usually works well with older students who have limited reading skills. It has the added benefit of teaching them something about comparison shopping and life skills at the same time. Bring to class the food pages from several newspapers. Show students how to locate advertisements, clip coupons, and organize them according to food groups and categories. Then help them make a simple shopping list using these coupons. After that, show them how to calculate the amount of money they will save by using the coupons. Encourage students to set up their own filing system for coupons and to use them when they go shopping with family members. Recently, I was delighted to hear that, as a result of our discussion and hands-on comparisons in the classroom, one student was able to convince her mother to start using double coupons at a local grocery store!

Learning About Nutrition

- Discuss the four food groups and, if possible, post a drawing of the pyramid of basic food groups and recommended daily helpings on the bulletin board. Compare and contrast the recommended diet with the students' own diets. Ask students

MATERIALS

✓ *a poster showing the official United States Department of Agriculture Food Pyramid, published in 1991*

to write a list of everything they ate the day before. Suggest that they organize it according to the number of servings in each group from the food pyramid.

- Then have them compare and contrast what they ate with what is listed in the pyramid. The final product, which involves reading, thinking, and writing, could be a collage of the various items they ate, contrasted with the recommended items. (Artistic students may want to draw their own pictures.) The final products can be shared with the rest of the class and then displayed in a prominent place in the classroom.

Activities for High Intermediate and Advanced Students

Research Projects. Some students may be ready to take on challenging research projects. Topics for such food-related projects might include:

- Food from Plants
- Food from Animals
- The Ten Most Nutritious Foods
- The Ten Least Nutritious Foods
- Junk Food or Healthy Snacks?
- World Hunger: Causes and Solutions

Becoming a Crop Expert. Ask students to sign up for one or two crops, preferably crops harvested in their country or local area. Have them research the crop, including its history and any legends or myths associated with it. One of my students found out that, according to a Mayan legend from Mexico, the first people were created out of corn. Another sixth grader chose to do her research on the goddess Ceres-Demeter, which tied in very neatly with the sixth-grade curriculum and program of studies.

Making Pie Graphs. As part of their research, have students use an encyclopedia and other reference books to look for data on the total production (or consumption) of one grain. They can choose wheat, rice, millet, etc. Students sharpen their math skills as they divide the pie-like circle into portions to represent their statistical findings. The colorful graphs of the major crops help students retain the information, which they like to share and discuss with their families. Thus, books and projects constitute powerful tools in involving family members in the thinking and acclimatization process.

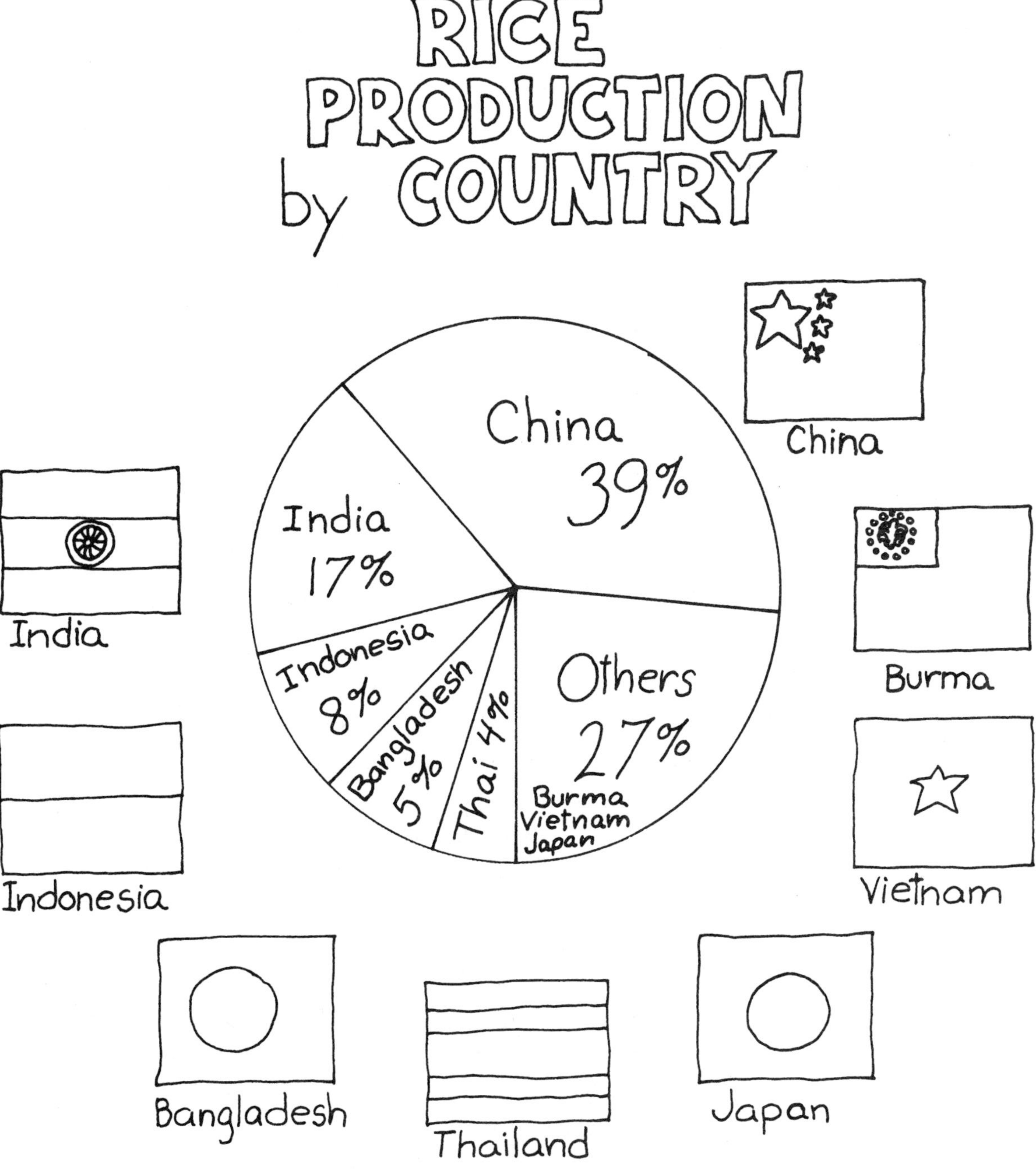

A Sample Pie Graph

GETTING FAMILIES INVOLVED

This unit literally constitutes food for thought. Very early on I acquaint family members with what is being taught in class, and invite them to participate in the process. For instance, all the webs started in class necessitate input from families, since many children attending elementary school remember little about life in their country of origin.

Family members may participate in contributing native dishes to a potluck supper. By the way, the notice sent home to tell families about upcoming projects or activities should be very explicit. A few years ago, one person apologized for not being able to bring china from her country. She had interpreted the term *native dish* literally, and after a good laugh, we both decided that, in the future, we would need to send home less ambiguous instructions, preferably in the students' native languages.

Potluck suppers and international festivals with food booths are immensely popular. They create good will for the whole school and, at the same time, foster global understanding. Regulations vary by state and county, so you will need to make sure that it is legal to ask students to bring food to school.

Putting Together a Class Cookbook

Compiling and editing hundreds of recipes contributed by enthusiastic family members is a formidable job, and you will need strong support from volunteers to embark upon such a project. Large index cards with holes punched in two or three places and gathered by key rings make attractive, practical cookbooks. A volunteer culinary expert should check ingredients, proportions, and cooking terms. Credit should be given to the contributors of each recipe, and mention of the countries they come from should also be included. Students, family members, even teachers can embellish each recipe with artful drawings.

In 1983, my colleague, Vincenzina DiPietro, and I compiled and edited the *Haycock E.S.L. International Cookbook* with some much-needed help from volunteers and with the staunch support from our Principal, Kay Wright. The 118-page cookbook includes such exotic dishes as *caponata* from Sicily, *cha gio* from South Vietnam, *grzyby ze smietan* (mushrooms in sour sauce) from Poland, *rempah* (sausage-coconut fritters) from Indonesia, *porta espanola* (a dessert) from Argentina, *mahn-doo* (a beef dish) from Korea, chicken in groundnut sauce from West Africa, and a spicy mint soup from Tibet, especially enjoyable on a cold winter night.

Displaying Cooking Utensils from Around the World

Ask students to get their families to help them find and share with the rest of the class any cooking utensils or appliances which are typical of their country of origin. After seeing such items as an old coffee grinder from France, a mortar and pestle from Africa, or a Laotian coconut grater, children will recognize how functional all these utensils are. They will also be better able to reflect on the importance of culinary traditions, and to understand the role played by climate and geography in the growing and preparing of foods.

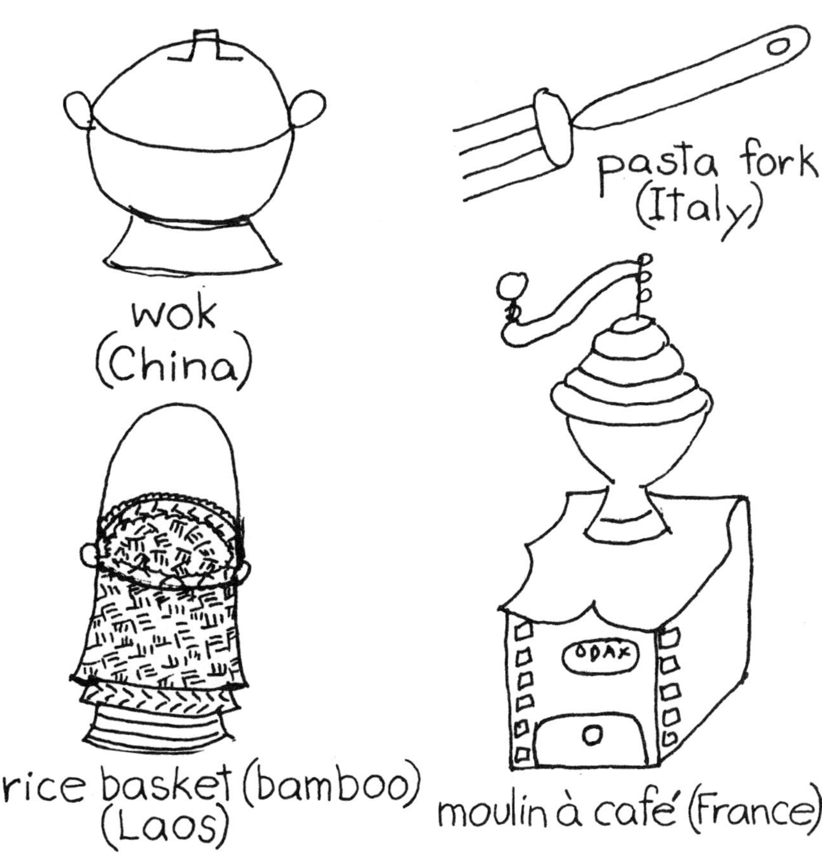

Illustrations by the author

CONCLUSION

This unit reinforces the concept of interconnectedness. Through daily discussions about food with you, with their peers, and with their families, students are developing vocabulary in a structured fashion, and learning to read. At the same time, they are also reading to learn—broadening their horizons as they research legends and myths from the past, look for facts from up-to-date reference materials, and project their thoughts into the future.

We can also use the topic of food to help them begin to think about the implications of global warming, the overuse of pesticides, and the needs of starving peoples. Above all, your discussions will nurture an understanding of the interdependence of all of us in our modern world, of the links between all beings, and of the need for cooperation among all people everywhere.

SUGGESTED READINGS

(Titles mentioned in this chapter are marked with a ◆.)

Aliki. *Green Grass and White Milk.* New York: Thomas Y. Crowell Company, 1986.

———. *The King's Day: Louis XIV of France.* New York: Harper Trophy, 1991. (France)

Ancona, George, *Bananas: From Manolo to Margie.* New York: Houghton Mifflin, 1982.

Bacon, Josephine. *Cooking the Israeli Way.* Minneapolis, Minnesota: Lerner Publishing Company, 1986. (Israel)

Bailey, Donna and Sproule, Anna. *Brazilian Festivals.* Austin, Texas: Steck-Vaughn Company, 1991. (Brazil)

◆ Barrett, Judy. *Cloudy With a Chance of Meatballs.* New York: Aladdin Books, 1982.

Barrett-Dragon, Patricia, and Dalton, Rosemary. *The Kid's Cookbook.* San Leandro, California: Bristol Publishing Enterprises, Inc., 1982.

◆ Bider, Djemma. *A Drop of Honey.* New York: Simon and Schuster Books for Young Readers, 1977.

- Burt, Olive. *Let's Find Out About Bread.* New York: Franklin Watts, Inc., 1966.
- Catling, Patrick. *The Chocolate Touch.* New York: Bantam Books, 1952.
- de Paola, Tomie. *Strega Nona.* Englewood Cliffs, New Jersey: Prentice-Hall Books for Young Readers, 1975. (Italy) (A Caldecott Honor Book)
- ———. *Watch Out for the Chicken Feet in Your Soup.* Englewood Cliffs, New Jersey: Prentice-Hall Books for Young Readers, 1974.
- Dooley, Norah. *Everybody Cooks Rice.* Minneapolis: Carolrhoda Books, 1987.
- Dorros, Arthur. *Tonight is Carnaval.* New York: Dutton Children's Books, 1991. (Peru)

Floethe, Louise and Richard. *Fishing Around the World.* New York: Charles Scribner's Sons, 1972.

Ford, B. G. *Don't Forget the Oatmeal! A Supermarket Word Book.* New York: Western Publishing Company, Inc., 1980.

Galbraith, Clare K. *Victor.* Boston: Little, Brown and Company, 1971.

Galdone, Paul. *The Magic Porridge Pot.* Boston: Houghton Mifflin, 1979.

- Grifalconi, Ann. *The Village of Round and Square Houses.* New York: Little, Brown and Co., 1986.

Hall, Tom. *The Golden Tombo.* New York: Alfred A. Knopf, 1959.

- Kaufman, Cheryl Davidson. *Cooking the Caribbean Way.* Minneapolis, Minnesota: Lerner Publishing Company, 1988. (the Caribbean)
- Lasky, Kathryn. *Sugaring Time.* New York: Aladdin Books, 1983. (A Newbery Honor Book)
- Lewis, Thomas P. *The Dragon Kite.* New York: Holt, Rinehart and Winston, 1974.

McCloskey, Robert. *Blueberries for Sal.* New York: Viking Press, 1948. (A Caldecott Honor Book) (Also available in a Penguin Books edition)

Milhous, Katherine. *The Egg Tree.* New York: Alladin Books, 1981.

- Mitchell, Barbara. *A Pocketful of Goobers.* Minneapolis: Carolrhoda Books, 1988. (African-American)
- Mitgutsch, Ali. *From Beet to Sugar.* Minneapolis: Carolrhoda Books, 1981.
- ———. *From Cacao Bean to Chocolate.* Minneapolis: Carolrhoda Books, 1981.
- Morris, Ann. *Bread Bread Bread.* New York: Lothrop, Lee and Shepard Books, 1989.
- Musgrove, Margaret. *From Ashanti to Zulu,* African Traditions. New York: Dial Books for Young Readers, 1977. (A Caldecott Medal Book)

Rhoads, Dorothy. *The Corn Grows Ripe.* New York: Viking Press, 1956. (Mayan Indians)

Sabin, Louis. *Colonial Life in America.* Mahwah, New Jersey: Troll Associates, 1985.

Seed, Jenny. *Ntombi's Song,* Boston: Beacon Press Books, Boston, 1989.

- Seuss, Dr. *Green Eggs and Ham.* New York: Random House Books for Young Readers, 1960

Shaw, Janet. *Kirsten's Surprise: A Christmas Story.* Madison, Wisconsin: The Pleasant Company, 1986.

Showers, Paul. *What Happens to a Hamburger?* New York: Thomas Y. Crowell Company, 1970. (available in Spanish)

Sullivan, Judith. *We Are Navajo.* New York: Harcourt Brace Jovanovich, 1976.

- Turner, Dorothy. *Bread.* Minneapolis: Carolrhoda Books, 1989. (1989 Outstanding Science Trade Book)

———. *Eggs.* Minneapolis: Carolrhoda Books, 1989.

———. *Milk.* Minneapolis: Carolrhoda Books, 1988. (1989 Outstanding Science Trade Book)

- Wilder, Laura Ingalls. *Little House in the Big Woods.* New York: Harper & Row, 1971.

SORTING FOODS

Name________________________________ Date ______________

Put the words in the right column.

Fruits	Vegetables	Other Foods
________	________	________
________	________	________
________	________	________
________	________	________
________	________	________
________	________	________
________	________	________
________	________	________
________	________	________
________	________	________
________	________	________
________	________	________
________	________	________
________	________	________
________	________	________
________	________	________

SWEET/SOUR CHART

Name________________________________ Date ______________

Food Bites	Sweet	Sour	Salty	Bitter
radish				
slice of lemon				
red apple				
pretzel				
horseradish				
taco chip				
strawberry				
slice of pickle or gherkin				

OPPOSITES

Name______________________________ Date _______________

Rana and Rouba are twins, but they do not have the same tastes. Fill in the blanks with opposites using adjectives from the Word Bank.

Example: **hot** cold

1. sweet ____________________
2. salty ____________________
3. fat ____________________
4. tasty ____________________
5. ripe ____________________
6. raw ____________________
7. fresh ____________________
8. tender ____________________
9. spicy ____________________
10. well-done ____________________

Word Bank

bland	sour
cooked	stale
lean	tasteless
mild	tough
rare	unripe

HAMUD'S BAG AND BASKET

Name______________________________ Date ______________

Hamud is helping his mother shop at the market. His job is to place all the mass nouns in the bag, and all the count nouns in the basket. Can you help him?

MARKET

apple		peach
apricot	guava	pepper
banana	lentils	plantain
bulgur wheat	milk	rice
cornmeal	millet	salt
grapefruit	orange	sugar
green pepper	papaya	tapioca

RUKHAMINI'S FAVORITE FRUIT

Name______________________________ Date ______________

Rukhamini lives in Ghat Kopar in India. She likes the monsoon season because she can go to her native village and eat her favorite fruit, the mango. Help Rukhamini put these nouns in plural form so she can eat as many as she wants.

Example: **mango** mangoes

1. cherry ________________
2. peach ________________
3. tomato ________________
4. radish ________________
5. strawberry ________________
6. potato ________________
7. blueberry ________________
8. avocado ________________
9. blackberry ________________
10. raspberry ________________

TABLE OF FACTS

Name______________________________ Date ______________

Weather and Climate	
Crops and Food	
Country Described	
Author and Illustrator	
Title of Book	